BORN TO PLAY

**Contributions to
the Study of Music and Dance**

BORN TO PLAY

The Life and Career of Hazel Harrison

Jean E. Cazort and
Constance Tibbs Hobson

CONTRIBUTIONS TO THE STUDY OF
MUSIC AND DANCE, NUMBER 3

GREENWOOD PRESS
WESTPORT, CONNECTICUT • LONDON, ENGLAND

Library of Congress Cataloging in Publication Data

Cazort, Jean E.
  Born to play.

  (Contributions to the study of music and dance,
ISSN 0193-9041 ; no. 3)
    Includes index.
    Bibliography: p.
    1. Harrison, Hazel, 1883-1969. 2. Pianists—United
States—Biography. I. Hobson, Constance Tibbs.
II. Title. III. Series.
ML417.H247C4   1983   786.1'092'4 [B]   82-12169
ISBN 0-313-23643-7

Library of Congress Catalog Card Number: 82-12169
ISBN: 0-313-23643-7
ISSN: 0193-9041

First published in 1983

Greenwood Press
A division of Congressional Information Service, Inc.
88 Post Road West, Westport, Connecticut 06881

Printed in the United States of America

10 9 8 7 6 5 4 3 2 1

Copyright Acknowledgments

Grateful acknowledgment is given for permission to use the following:

The article "Pianist Plays Bach, Liszt and Busoni" by Glenn Dillard Gunn, which
appeared in the *Washington Times Herald* on January 4, 1954.

Articles which appeared in the *La Porte Daily Herald* on September 21, 1911;
October 31, 1914; and November 10, 1914.

Every reasonable effort has been made to trace the owners of copyright materials
used in this book, but in some instances this has proven impossible. The publisher
will be glad to receive information leading to more complete acknowledgment in
subsequent printings of this book and in the meantime extends its apologies for any
omissions.

To Ralph

To Craig

CONTENTS

ILLUSTRATIONS

PREFACE

Hazel Harrison is a name to ponder over. She was one of the legendary pianists of the twentieth century. Persons who heard her play, perhaps fifty years ago, still rhapsodize over the experience. She succeeded as a concert artist when the twin obstacles of race and sex were mighty forces against it. Her students idolized her. Because her devotion to her art was all-consuming, it was often her students who assisted her in the mundane chores of daily life and saw to her comfort in later years. She was the undisputed "premiere pianiste of the colored race" for almost four decades.

Yet the mention of her name today to generally knowledgeable persons is likely to draw a blank. Except for a brief discussion in Maud Cuney Hare's *Negro Musicians and Their Music* (1936) and, more recently, in Eileen Southern's *The Music of Black Americans* (1971), Raoul Abdul's *Blacks in Classical Music* (1977), and Geneva Southall's *Blind Tom* (1979), little has been written about Hazel Harrison. Josephine Harreld Love's article about her in *Notable American Women, The Modern Period* (1980) is the most complete discussion to date of Harrison's life and career.

No publication has dealt definitively with her as a person and as an artist. Many of those who knew her best have died. The authors present this volume in the hope that it will reaffirm her place in the galaxy of great performers of this century and will introduce to those who have not heard of her the pleasure of her company.

ACKNOWLEDGMENTS

The authors are indeed grateful to all who aided in bringing the story of Hazel Harrison to light. While it would be impossible to name all the persons from whom we received help—which in no way lessens our gratitude to them—we wish to mention several for their singular cooperation and assistance.

We are indebted to the staffs of libraries and of other repositories for their invaluable assistance in obtaining information and materials: the Moorland-Spingarn Research Center of Howard University, particularly Michael R. Winston, director, Thomas C. Battle, curator of manuscripts, Esme E. Bhan, manuscript research associate, Janet Sims Wood, reference librarian, and Dorothy Porter Wesley, retired curator; the Fine Arts Library, Howard University, with especial thanks to Carrie B. Hackney, librarian; the Library of Congress, especially Elmer Booze of the Music Division; the Schomburg Center for Research in Black Culture; the Martin Luther King Public Library, Washington, D.C.; the Azalia Hackley Collection of the Detroit Public Library; Daniel Williams, archivist, Tuskegee Institute; and E. Juel Troy, former reference librarian of the La Porte Public Library.

We are grateful to the former students, colleagues, and friends of Hazel Harrison who responded so graciously to requests for correspondence, pictures, and information: Louise Burge, Chester Rowlett, Sterling Thomas; and to the persons who granted interviews, listed below.

To relatives, colleagues, friends, and students, whose support and encouragement were so helpful, a special word of thanks: Doris E. McGinty of Howard University; Jessie Carney Smith of Fisk University; Edith Work and Thyckla Johnson of Nashville; Ethel Moore of La Grange, Georgia; Victor Partridge and Roy Hill of Atlanta; Marcia Elder of Bedford, Massachusetts; Dominique-René de Lerma of Morgan State University; and Florence Andrew of La Porte.

Finally, special measures of gratitude go to husband Ralph Cazort and to son Craig Hobson for their willingness to log thousands of driving miles and meet airline and bus schedules, and for their patience and encouragement, which assured the completion of the work.

TAPE-RECORDED INTERVIEWS
(unless otherwise noted)

Lillian M. Allen (not taped)
William Duncan Allen
Marian Allman
Reva Allman
Robert Earl Anderson
Florence Andrew
Edward Boatner
Ralph Bryson
Mrs. Osborne Chambliss
William E. Dawson (not taped)
Louise Fargher (telephone)
Elizabeth Foster
Paul Gary
Frederick Hall
Mildred Greenwood Hall
Alfonso Harrod
Lawrence Hayes
Frances White Hughes
Hermine Johnigan
Raymond Johnson
Josephine Harreld Love
Laura McCray
Frances Sampson Mask
William Mitchell
Geraldine Nesbitt

Minnie Scott
Grennetta Simpson
Ralph Simpson
Florence Low Stoner
Althea Thomas
Benjamin Ward
Esther Wroten (not taped)

PRELUDE

The crowd in the Arena Auditorium was both expectant and curious. It had forgotten the discomfort of getting there in the February afternoon drizzle. There was not an empty seat in the 1,600-seat auditorium. Those who had heard her play before knew what a great musical experience was in store for them, but they weren't sure whether the grande dame of the piano could still pull it off.

"How old *is* she? She must be eighty if she's a day!"

"How's she going to play the piano? She can hardly walk!"

"My husband fixed her up a little potion so she can walk. I hope she took it."

The stage in the Arena Auditorium at Alabama State College was decorated with flowers. The lights were lowered, and the audience became quiet. All eyes were waiting for Hazel Harrison to make her appearance. And suddenly, there she was, walking onstage, surely and regally, wearing a pea-green gown, and bowing in response to the surging waves of applause that greeted her. It was an expression of love and respect for this great artist who had become a legend in her own time. The bond between the audience and the performer was firmly fixed even before the first note was sounded. Instinctively, the audience knew that its doubts about her had been groundless.

From the first note, the old magic took over, and the audience sat, spellbound, as she played the "Song of the Lute" by Respighi, Prelude and Fugue by Sgambati, the Liszt B Minor Sonata, three short etudes of Jelobinsky, and Rachmaninoff's "Moment Musical no. 4." And of special interest was the premiere of a piece written especially for her by a young colleague, entitled "Presentiment."

At the close of the program the ovation was thunderous. Flowers were presented. She played an encore: the Schulz-Evler arrangement of the "Blue Danube" by Johann Strauss, which had become so closely associated with her, almost like a theme song. After another encore the recital was over. Those who had come from Tuskegee and from La Grange, Georgia, would return home, and the Montgomery residents would return to their homes, but they were all subdued and awed by the experience. It was a piano recital seldom equalled in Montgomery, and few others would evoke the same majesty from the college's newly acquired Baldwin piano.

Her career had now spanned sixty years, and here, in Alabama in 1959, this may have been her last major recital. Her musical beginnings went back to another time, when Brahms was still alive and Stravinsky had yet to compose his watershed *Rite of Spring*, when names such as d'Albert, Joachim, and Scharwenka dominated the concert scene.

That was the world Hazel Harrison had entered, to leave her mark in the years to come as one of the most distinguished pianists of the century.

BORN TO PLAY

1

THE LA PORTE YEARS: 1883-1911

La Porte, Indiana, in the 1880s was a good place to be born. It was an attractive and well-cared-for town in northern Indiana, only seventy-three miles east of Chicago and connected to it by boat and by train. But those miles in between consisted of woods and open country—or open water—and La Porte flourished on its own. Its citizens numbered about six thousand, and the whole face of the town bore the marks of good taste and industry.

A variety of tradesmen served its needs, and a large segment of its economic base came from farming the productive land around La Porte. The La Porte Carriage Company made buggies, surreys, and farm wagons; the La Porte Sash and Door Company made windows and doors; and the Great Western Company produced bicycles that were popular until the Depression. Harnesses of all types were made by the Lonns on Main Street. C. B. Way & Sons sold farm machinery and had a "tie shed" for farm horses when the owners came to town and the horses needed shelter from the weather.[1] Later, the Hobart M. Cable Piano Company moved its factory from Chicago to La Porte, thus providing succeeding generations of young piano pupils everywhere with their only knowledge of La Porte: "Hobart M. Cable, La Porte, Indiana" etched into their memories forever by the gold lettering on the nameboard. The streets of La Porte were wide and lined with trees. Overall, the town presented an appearance of late nineteenth-century comfort and stability, and its townspeople were proud of it.

This was the La Porte that Hazel Lucile Harrison was born into on

May 12, 1883, the only child of Hiram Nathaniel and Olive Jane Wood Harrison. Hiram was twenty-nine at the time. He had been born in Michigan and was descended from Cherokee Indians. Her mother, known to everyone as "Birdie," was twenty-four, and she had been born in Windsor, Canada.[2] Beyond that, little is known of the history of Hazel's family.

Since the Civil War, the black citizens of La Porte had never numbered more than fifty or so of those six thousand persons who made up its population. This was in marked contrast to La Porte's nearby neighbor, Michigan City, whose black population had always been much larger. The La Porte blacks had arrived there under several sets of circumstances. In the 1830s a few families had moved to La Porte with colored persons in their household service; others arrived later via the Underground Railroad. In the 1860s twenty-seven black families were brought to La Porte by the United States government to construct a railroad. They were settled on what is now Pulaski Street and were paid nine dollars a month. They had apparently lived as a settlement, with their own church and school, but they must have moved on when the construction was completed or when the war was over, as La Porte points very proudly to its record that its black citizens have always lived in different parts of the city and were never segregated.[3]

The Harrisons lived at 1306 Clay Street, in a two-story wooden house whose main architectural feature consisted of two French windows opening onto a front porch. The inside was roomy and very serviceable, and included a dining room with a large fireplace, a pump in the kitchen, and a large room behind the kitchen with a trapdoor to the basement. Upstairs were three rooms and a large attic.[4] Down the street lived the violin maker, Launer.

Hiram worked as a barber, an occupation that was followed by many blacks of the day. It apparently provided a respectable living, and he continued it as a main source of income, becoming, by 1884, co-proprietor of Stevens and Harrison, barbers on Main Street in downtown La Porte. Later, as the town grew and its postal service expanded to nearby farms and communities, Hiram Harrison became one of its first rural mail carriers. The other early black families in La Porte—the Sampsons, the Stewarts, the Adamses— were variously engaged as barber, milliner, seamstress, and proprietor of a Turkish bath. Boler Banks, who also owned a barbershop, was an active citizen who served as councilman from the Third Ward in the 1890s.

Olive Harrison must have felt the need to be more gainfully occupied herself, and she operated a beauty shop in the family home, where the ladies of La Porte and their daughters had their hair washed and arranged. She ran a classified ad continually in the *La Porte Daily Herald* over several years in the 1890s for "switches and waves made to order." One La Porte resident remembered how Olive Harrison wove, from human hair, an exquisite wig for her doll. Also, Olive may have suspected the extent of her daughter's talent, in which case additional money would be needed for lessons and related expenses.

Older citizens of La Porte still recall "Hi" Harrison's fine tenor voice when he sang as a choir member and soloist with the First Presbyterian Church, where he also played the piano for the Sunday school. The other black families attended the Catholic, Episcopal, and Baptist churches. Some years later, the black Methodist minister from Michigan City tried without success to get them to attend his own church, but the social climate of La Porte was amenable, and there was no need for them to change.[5]

Hazel's unusual musical gifts became evident at an early age. In a brief biographical sketch, which she prepared many years later, Hazel recalled that her music lessons began when she was about five and she had to be lifted onto the stool. When her father would get up to dress early in the morning, she would arise also and practice until school time. Her first music teacher was Richard Pellow, an Englishman who taught music in the La Porte schools and who served as organist for the First Presbyterian Church. He would tell her, "I will give you a penny for every perfect lesson that you have." And she would always have them perfect.[6]

By 1895, when she was twelve, Hazel had already acquired a significant local reputation, and she appeared on programs that boasted La Porte's finest talent. One of the big events in La Porte every summer was the annual Pine Lake Assembly, a Chautauqua-like program that lasted for several days, featuring preaching, hymn singing, and general moral uplift. Its musicales provided a showcase for local musicians, and in August 1895 Hazel appeared in a duet with her teacher, Richard Pellow, as well as in a solo performance. The local newspaper urged everyone to attend because the grounds were easily accessible by carriage, hack line, or steamboat.

In its review of the event, the *La Porte Daily Herald* (7 August 1895) reported that "it was the best musical program ever given in the auditorium. The largest audience, or one of the largest, that has thus far gathered during the present Assembly meeting greeted the array of talent selected for the occasion. . . . The musicale was under the direction of Prof. R. W. Pellow." Opening the program was a duet, "Tarantella," by Raff, played by Hazel and her teacher. After a half dozen violin selections and a reading, Hazel appeared again, this time as soloist, in Raff's "La Fileuse." The reviewer noted that "the audience was a very enthusiastic one," and would have liked encores, "but the performers . . . contented themselves with simply bowing in response."

The next summer she was again the star attraction of the Pine Lake Assembly musicale. By now, Hazel's musical gift was well known, and she enjoyed sharing it. In January 1897, when she was thirteen, she provided the musical background for one of La Porte's "swell social functions"—the winter ball of the Occidental Club. Throughout the evening, an "infectious spirit of delight" prevailed as "Miss Hazel Harrison, the pianist of the evening, caused the fair guests to revel in melody, soft and sweet, during the time that cards were the diversion." A late supper was served at 10 P.M., and dancing began at midnight, with Hazel providing the music for a grand march, followed by alternating waltzes and quadrilles, until 2 A.M.[7] The following Christmas, at another society function, the Union Club's charity ball, Birdie served as a maid, welcoming the guests as they arrived and seeing to their comfort.[8] All three of the Harrisons—Hiram, Birdie, and Hazel—were well liked and integrated into the community life of La Porte, and they all gave freely of their talents.

The Harrisons were also integrated in the community in another sense, a sense that the word did not take on until many decades later. The comfortable northern Indiana town provided insularity from the starker social realities of the outside world, not only for the Harrisons, but for all its citizens. As far as it can be determined, being black in La Porte never seemed to be a factor in Hazel's life. All her friends, as well as many of her parents' associates, were white. The young man who escorted her to the senior social was white. The Harrisons were prominent citizens and were frequently mentioned in the newspaper, but never as being "colored." When an 1899 burglary at their home was reported on page one of the *Daily Herald* (14 April 1899), it was noted that during the time of the robbery, Mrs. Hiram Harrison had gone to the home of a customer, Mr. Harrison was at his barber shop, and "Miss Hazel was at school."

Hazel's realization of her racial identity came when she was an adolescent. One day, on an outing at Michigan City with several of her friends, she saw a Negro and exclaimed, "There's one!" and shortly afterward, exclaimed again, "There's another one!" Her friends finally said to her, "Well, *you're* one, too!"[9] Hiram and Birdie did maintain social contacts in South Bend, presumably black, and attended social functions there. At one of the Friday afternoon meetings of the La Porte Reading Circle, Birdie read a paper entitled "Division in the Methodist Episcopal Church on Account of Slavery."[10]

No dance in La Porte was really complete unless Hazel provided the dance music. From when she began this sideline of playing for dances at the age of thirteen until her serious commitment to a concert career ruled it out, she was always in great demand. Whether it was a dancing party of about twenty couples at Lay's Hall with a program of two-steps and waltzes or at the outdoor dance pavilion at Weller's Grove, everyone agreed that Hazel furnished "charming music," the belles and beaux causing the dance floor to "fairly glisten with flying feet" as two-steps prevailed throughout the evening.[11] Her own fondness for dancing and her good humor no doubt completed the festive atmosphere of the dances.

By this time, Professor Victor Heinze of Chicago, former pupil of Theodor Leschetizsky and Ignacy Jan Paderewski, was coming to La Porte regularly to give music lessons. In February 1895, a notice appeared in the newspaper of a recital by his pupils. Perhaps it was on one of those occasions that Pellow asked Heinze to hear Hazel play. Hazel recalled that "he was very pleased; he had visions of me playing in Germany with an orchestra and he, Heinze, conducting."[12] Heinze married Fannie Andrew of La Porte and moved to his wife's hometown. Notices in the *Daily Herald* in 1895 (2, 4, 5, 6, 7 September 1895) called the public's attention to the fact that

"Mr. Victor Heinze will commence his piano instructions in this city on Monday, September 9. At the same time he will begin a course in theory, etc. of music." The price for a thirty-minute private lesson with Heinze was two dollars. It must have been about this time that Hazel became his pupil.

Hazel's association with Heinze was a turning point for her. It was Heinze who made her aware of her own enormous potential, of the future that could await her. Certainly it was one of the great good fortunes of history that the paths of the famous pianist and pedagogue, on the one hand, and the extremely talented Hazel, on the other, converged at this point. He carefully nurtured the young Hazel's artistic development and began to have grand conceptions of her performing with an orchestra in Germany and of her eventual concert career. His later affiliation with the Cosmopolitan School of Music and Dramatic Art provided the proper vehicle for Chicago audiences to hear his pupil perform regularly. There is an account of Heinze's taking her to hear the eminent Ferruccio Busoni in recital in Chicago. After the program, he took her backstage to meet Busoni, who listened to her play and said to her, "Now, little girl, you are very, very talented. Now, what I want you to do is this: I want you to work on technique. I want you to work on technique endlessly. In the meantime I want you to finish your school and as soon as you finish your high school, let me know, because I want you to come to Europe."[13]

Hazel had finished the "eighth and a half grade" in June 1898, the exercises having taken place in a schoolroom decorated with three large American flags. There were two piano solos: Gertrude Keuhne playing the Schubert-Liszt "Hark, Hark the Lark," and Hazel playing the Chopin Ballade opus 23. A vocal trio rendered "Down in the Dewey Dell," and R. W. Pellow accompanied the class songs.[14] Four years later, in 1902, she was graduated from La Porte High School.

The spring of 1902 had been a busy one for Hazel: a Studebaker Hall recital in Chicago that March,[15] playing for the dancing lessons given in La Porte by a Chicago dancing master,[16] and preparing her senior paper entitled "Liszt, the Pianist, and Schumann, the Composer."[17] Graduation events were spread over three days. On June 6 the junior class gave a reception for the senior class, transforming a large hallway in the high-school building. It was "festooned with myrtle, caught up by bouquets of daisies, and the broad stairways and landings decorated with rugs, potted and cut flowers, ferns and palms, and cozy corners abundantly supplied with chairs and sofa cushions." In the assembly room, a large stage with scenes and curtains had been built, and two one-act comedies were presented by the juniors, "The Smith Mystery" and "The Boston Dip."[18] On June 8 the baccalaureate service took place at Hall's Opera House. The stage, decorated with potted plants and flags, was occupied by officiating clergymen, the choir, the School Board, and the high-school faculty. There were appropriate hymns and a sermon.[19] And on June 12, commencement day, there were girls in white dresses, boys in white duck trousers, flowers, flags, music, cheers, applause, and a commencement address; and it was all over.[20]

After graduation, Hazel became a full-time piano teacher in La Porte, a profession for which her training, talent, and experience certainly qualified her. Added qualifications were her genuine warmth and her interest in others. Those were qualities on which people would comment for decades to come, and her generosity in giving of herself has become a part of the Hazel legend. She attracted and kept large numbers of piano pupils, continuing to live at home on Clay Street and giving her lessons there as well. That December she gave four recitals of her own, including one at the Heinze School of Artistic Piano Playing.

As a piano teacher, Hazel was not in competition with Heinze. His marriage to Fannie Andrew had not been successful, and he had moved back to Chicago.[21] Her fees were the same as his: two dollars for a half-hour lesson or three dollars for an hour's lesson.[22] Florence Andrew, one of her earliest pupils and a cousin of Fannie, recalls going to the Harrison home for lessons.

There was a small entrance hall, then the music room where the Hobart M. Cable upright was. Directly back of that was her mother's beauty parlor. "Beauty parlor" we called it; it was just a separate room which had a nice dresser with mirror. Then beyond that was a kitchen. I never went out in the kitchen. I can hear Hazel now, saying, "Birdie, have you put on the beans?" She was quite explosive. I remember one day striking a wrong note and she said, "Oh, did I scare you?" She was that way. And she'd follow me out and say, "Now, Florence, practice, practice!"[23]

Although her responsibilities as a piano teacher took up much of
her time, Hazel continued her own heavy practice schedule. She
commuted weekly to Chicago for lessons with Heinze, and was
making long-range plans for her career. There was to be no more
playing for dances until 2 A.M., but she did engage in some
recreational music making. La Porte boasted two other musicians
of great promise: Helen Poole and Otto Meyer. Helen Poole,
several years older than either Meyer or Hazel, frequently appeared
on church programs and at civic events. She was *the* outstanding
singer in La Porte and possessed a lovely soprano voice. Later, she
became music director of the La Porte public schools. Otto Meyer
was a violinist of great ability and also a pupil of Victor Heinze.
They all enjoyed playing together and, in the spring of 1903,
decided to give a concert for the citizens of La Porte. They rented
Lay's Hall, scheduled the concert for May 29, and, even though the
concert was announced only a few days beforehand, it was
attended by a large audience. The *Daily Herald* (29 May 1903)
reported that it could be "truthfully said that few if any cities in
Indiana the size of La Porte could present such an array of talent."
Otto Meyer played several solo violin pieces and Helen Poole sang
an aria from *Samson et Dalila* and some additional pieces, but
Hazel's participation was confined on this occasion to accompanying. The three of them—soprano, violin, and piano—
performed Mascheroni's "For All Eternity," "the trio forming a
bewitching combination, the effect of which was instantly noticed
on the audience, who went into raptures over the number." The
"exquisite music rendered" was "an artistic triumph in praise of
which too much cannot be said."

On November 2, 1903, the *Daily Herald* carried in the center of
page one the announcement that Hazel and Heinze had been
working so hard for:

GREAT HONOR AWAITS HER

La Porte's Gifted Pianist Will Probably Appear in Berlin

As Soloist with the Philharmonic Orchestra

Prof. Victor Heinze Planning Brilliant Tour for Miss Hazel
Harrison, Whose Wonderful Playing Has Brought Her Many
Encomiums from Musicians and Critics in This Country

Although negotiations had not been completed, it was anticipated that Hazel would go to Berlin in September and appear as a soloist with the Philharmonic Orchestra at the Royal Theater. It was considered the greatest possible honor that could be bestowed on any pianist because the Philharmonic was considered to be without peer. The article mentioned that "Miss Harrison has played before the most exacting musical critics in Chicago and other cities and has been showered with praises, and recently she played from memory, as soloist with the Metropolitan Orchestra, a selection of eighty-seven pages, the people going into raptures over the performance."

With her goal in view, Hazel rededicated herself and intensified her preparation, if that could have been possible. She continued with her pupils, but she absolutely eliminated other activities. Only once did she break her self-imposed discipline: to help the Women's Literary Society celebrate its twenty-sixth anniversary with a presentation of *A Midsummer Night's Dream* at the Andrew home. Presiding at the piano, Hazel had both the score and the libretto before her, playing snatches of the music as passages were read. It was "of very fine execution, and *con expressione* which touched the feelings."[24] The audience enjoyed it all the more, realizing that it was their last opportunity for a while, as Hazel was preparing a final recital before her departure in September.

In Hazel's day, a European appearance was all but obligatory for any American musician seriously aspiring to a concert career. Success at home almost demanded it, and the Berlin papers were filled with notices of aspiring young American performers, some to become famous and others to be forgotten the very next day:

Ten Americans concertized here during the three months, to wit: Paris Chambers, Michael von Zadora, Minnie Coons, Ruth L. Dego, Celeste Groenvelt, Ernest Schelling, Bessie Silberfeld, Patrick O'Sullivan, Max Pilzer and Albert Zimmer. . . .[25]

Bessie Silberfeld, a little American girl . . . dresses and long curls, made her Berlin debut.[26]

Minnie Coons, an American, made her debut . . . accompanied by the Leipsic Philharmonic Orchestra under the direction of her teacher, Xaver Scharwenka.[27]

Among American students is Reginald Hidden, the violinist.[28]

In the American colony great interest was centered in the debut of the young San Francisco pianist, Irwin Eveleth Hassel.[29]

Aid to a few of these young artists came through the auspices of the Wolff Musical Bureau, which had founded a new series

for the purpose of helping to a public appearance in the German capital gifted young artists who are unknown and who have not the means to give concerts of their own. Four concerts will be given in the Philharmonie with the Philharmonic Orchestra. At each two hitherto unknown young soloists will appear, and further, as a drawing card, a soloist of world renown.[30]

Hazel's appearance in Berlin may have been under different arrangements, especially since she was not to share the evening with anyone. But whatever the details, Hazel's dream had now become a reality, and La Porte was bursting with pride. The appearance carried no financial award, but it greatly enhanced a young artist's chances of success. In addition to the appearance with the Philharmonic, there were to be recitals in Berlin and in other parts of Germany, where she would appear under the auspices of the orchestra.[31]

The long-anticipated appearance in Berlin was scheduled for October 22, 1904, with the celebrated Nikisch conducting.[32] But before leaving La Porte, Hazel planned to give a farewell concert at Hall's Opera House on May 23, which would give her ample time for final preparation and would serve as a "dry run" for some of the pieces she was preparing. Appearing with her on the program would be Leon Marx, violinist, who would be accompanied by Victor Heinze.[33]

When the day of the concert arrived, the *Daily Herald* (23 May 1904) announced that two La Porte clubs, the Charity Club and the O.N.T. (Our Night Together) would gather at the home of one of the members and attend the concert in a body. In addition, the paper reminded its readers that the concert would begin promptly at eight o'clock, and that persons coming after that hour would be required to stand in the lobby until the number being played had been completed.

Hazel's program for that evening, which the newspaper referred

to in its review as one of "classical severity," opened with a Bach
Prelude and Fugue, followed by the Schumann Sonata in G Minor,
five Chopin études, an arrangement of Johann Strauss's "Tales
from the Vienna Woods," and Moszkowski's "Caprice Espagnol."
Interspersed were the violin selections played by Leon Marx and
accompanied by Victor Heinze. The reviewer was plainly moved by
the event, and wrote of its impact not only on him, but on Hazel as
well:

Last evening at 8 o'clock must have been the proudest moment of Miss
Hazel Lucile Harrison's life. Not that she had not been honored before,
not that she had not rendered classical musical programs before, not that
she had not appeared before musical connoisseurs previously, not that she
had not been applauded, been honored, and received ovations before, but
those triumphs were not before her neighbors and friends and schoolmates,
the friends of her school girl days, her boon companions and ardent
admirers, and last, but not least, her parents and other relatives.

He continued, noting that

no sincerer tribute could have been paid anyone than was bestowed on Miss
Harrison last evening by the culture and wealth of La Porte, the people of
her home town—the place where she was born and in which she has grown
to womanhood—who have known her from her babyhood till this hour,
who have watched her musical unfolding, the budding of her genius,
encouraged her in her efforts and rejoiced at her triumphs.

For the occasion, she was dressed in "modest attire, with no
adornment of flower or medal, or anything which could bear even
silent testimony to the marvelous musical skill that for the nonce
was quiescent in those well-trained fingers and that musical soul."
Whatever embarrassment may have existed on her part disappeared
as she approached the instrument "on which she was to exert her
power, and record her skill, and from which she was to evolve those
harmonious sounds with which the auditorium soon became
filled," and a sympathy between the artist and the audience became
plainly visible. Regarding her playing, he wrote:

There was a sparkle about everything she did. . . . The pure tone, the
correct intonation, the admirable phrasing, the poetry and the prose, in
short the fine sense of musical proportion, stamped on the girlish artist as a

real musical genius of whom her relatives, friends, acquaintances and townspeople have the greatest reason to be proud.

The article further noted that portions of the program were the same as would be given in each of the six programs to be rendered by Miss Harrison at the Philharmonic Orchestra concerts, to be given in Berlin and other parts of Germany, where she would appear under the auspices of the orchestra. The concert had been sponsored as a benefit for Hazel, and the amount realized from box-office receipts was nearly $500.[34]

* * *

Berlin in the first decade of the twentieth century was a musical mecca. Its artistic and cultural climate was rich with fare of the highest order. The new Berlin correspondent for the *Musical Courier* had just arrived from New York in January 1904, and he reported that the second half of the concert season was in full swing and that no fewer than twelve violinists had given recitals during the previous week.[35] By April he reported:

Fully 350 concerts [were] given here during the second half of the season, since January. Glancing backward we find that there were some eighty piano recitals of celebrities . . . Godowsky, Carreño, d'Albert, Schnabel . . . Gabrilowitsch . . . Scharwenka . . . which have been heard. The piano compositions played were mostly standard works. A new departure was made by Leopold Godowsky, who gave a Schumann recital, and with great success. . . . There were some promising debutants but none that made an extraordinary impression.

A partial listing of concertos played with the orchestra included Beethoven (E-flat Major, G Major, C Minor), Weber ("Concert-stück"), Brahms (D Minor and B-flat Major), Tschaikowsky, Rubinstein (D Minor), Grieg, Chopin (E Minor), Schumann, Pugno, Schutte, Saint-Saëns (C Minor), Liszt (E-flat Major and A Major), Mendelssohn (G Minor), Stevenhagen, d'Albert (E Major), and Meckel.[36]

Drama was flourishing as well: the Opera and the Royal Schauspielhaus were devoted to classical drama; the Deutsches Theater was presenting performances of Hauptmann, Ibsen, and Tolstoy;

and Max Reinhardt was introducing Strindberg to German audiences.[37] A new theater was to be built at a cost of 2,600,000 marks.[38] The opera subscription concerts, conducted by Felix Weingartner, were the highlight of the Berlin season.[39] A new building for the Berlin Royal Opera had been approved, and the sum of 50,000 marks had been granted for the necessary preparatory work.[40]

Hermann Wolff, the famous impresario, was presenting to the Berlin public the foremost singers, pianists, and violinists of the day. The great Nikisch was at the helm of the Berlin Philharmonic. Pianists Arthur Schnabel, Paderewski, Eugen d'Albert, and Ossip Gabrilowitsch (later the conductor of the Detroit Symphony) were regularly appearing before the critical and musically knowledgeable Berlin public. Young Arthur Rubinstein was completing his musical education in the city and had been presented by Hermann Wolff the year before.[41] Possibly the greatest pianist of them all, Ferruccio Busoni, whom Rubinstein called "the most interesting pianist alive . . . the awe-inspiring master of them all,"[42] was living in Berlin, giving solo recitals, and conducting orchestral concerts.

The week of October 16, 1904, began in the usual fashion. There were concerts daily in each of the famous concert halls—names so familiar to the music lovers of Berlin: Bechstein Hall, Beethoven Hall, Singakademie, Philharmonie, Philharmonie Small Hall, and the opera houses: Royal, West Side, and National. The calendar was full and the offerings varied, as the following schedule of weekly events will show:[43]

Monday October 17

Bechstein Hall	Gottfried Galston, piano
Beethoven Hall	Contemporary Composers' concert
Philharmonie	Philharmonic Chorus (Siegfried Ochs)
Royal Opera	*Magic Flute*
West Side Opera	*Postillon von Lonjumeau*
National Opera	*Freischütz*

Tuesday, October 18

Bechstein Hall	Marianne de Maringh, vocal
Beethoven Hall	Berthe Marx-Goldschmidt, piano
Singakademie	Martha Schley, vocal
Philharmonie	Philharmonic "Pop"
Philharmonie Small Hall	Eva Uhlmann, vocal
Emperor William Memorial Church	Sacred concert
Royal Opera	Opera symphony concert
West Side Opera	*Die Kleinen Lämmer*
National Opera	*Barber of Seville* (Bonci)

Wednesday, October 19

Bechstein Hall	Otto Silhavy, violin Margarete Weissbach, vocal
Beethoven Hall	Matja von Niessen-Stone, vocal
Philharmonie Hall	Philharmonic "Pop"
Philharmonie Small Hall	Erica von Binzer, piano
Singakademie	Julius Marton, vocal
American Church	Edwin A. Kraft, organ concert
Royal Opera	*Bajazzi, Coppelia*
West Side Opera	*Traviata*
National Opera	*Figaro's Hochzeit*

Thursday, October 20

Bechstein Hall	Martha Sauvan, piano
Beethoven Hall	Martha Drews, violin with Philharmonic Orchestra
Philharmonie	Franz von Vecsey, violin
Singakademie	Barth Madrigal Vereinigung
Royal Opera	*Robert the Devil*

West Side Opera	*Die Kleinen Lämmer*
National Opera	*Rigoletto* (with Bonci as the Duke)

Friday, October 21

Bechstein Hall	Hollander Quartet
Beethoven Hall	Henry Marteau, violin Willy Rehberg, piano
Philharmonie	Erk Male Chorus
Singakademie	Robert F. Mannereich, vocal
Philharmonie Small Hall	Fritz Binder, piano Richard Kroemer, violin Fritz Becker, 'cello
Royal Opera	*Flying Dutchman*
West Side Opera	*Die Kleinen Lämmer*
National Opera	*Figaro's Hochzeit*

Saturday, October 22

Bechstein Hall	Maikki Järnefeldt, vocal
Beethoven Hall	Bohemian Quartet (assisted by Arthur Schnabel, pianist)
Philharmonie Small Hall	Sergei von Bortkiewicz, piano
Singakademie	Hazelda Harrison, piano, with Philharmonic Orchestra
Royal Opera	*Hänsel und Gretel, Coppelia*
West Side Opera	*William Tell*
National Opera	Bonci in *Rigoletto*, Act IV; *Barber of Seville*, Act II; *La Favorita*, Act IV

Hazel's big appearance was on Saturday, October 22 at the Singakademie, where she played two piano concertos: the Chopin E Minor and the Grieg A Minor. Although Nikisch was originally scheduled to conduct, the concert was in fact conducted by August Scharrer. There is no doubt that this was Hazel's most important appearance to date, and ever afterward it was always referred to as the high-water mark in her career. Twenty-seven years earlier, in 1877, the Fisk Jubilee Singers had appeared at the Singakademie. They wrote in their diary:

Our interpreter, Mr. Kuistermaker, had said that a number of the greatest musical critics, before whom all the great singers appeared, were to be present, and if we failed we would better pack our trunks and leave. So when we stood before these gentlemen (critics) all of them on the front seat, (the worst place from which to judge us) we trembled.[44]

Hazel, no doubt, suffered similar apprehension, but once she faced the audience, saw their faces, and heard the enthusiastic applause, she knew that she had won. The audience was in evening dress, and many persons came up afterward to congratulate her.

The reviews were cordial and complimentary, making note of her extreme youth (she was actually twenty-one) and holding out great promise for her future. The *Deutscher Reichsanzeiger* felt that Hazelda Harrison showed "great talent and excellent technic. Quite especially beautiful and soft is her 'piano,' while one could have wished for a little more strength in the 'forte' places. Her playing does not reveal personal conception and independence, but it shows so much musical intelligence that we are justified in expecting much from her further development."[45] *Tageblatt* reported that "although the youthful pianist, Hazelda Harrison, has not yet a wholly matured art conception, she compensated for the lack of this in a sense by her universally smooth flowing technic."[46] The *German Times* commented on her "sympathetic touch and an unusually nice cantabile";[47] *Die Post* remarked on her delivery, which "revealed feeling and individuality and her technical ability bespoke thorough schooling."[48]

Birdie collected the reviews and sent them back to friends in La Porte who were anxious to know how Hazel had been received. The *Daily Herald* (15 November 1904) reflected the proud reaction of the townspeople when it wrote that there was "just enough adverse criticism in the accounts, which were written by the musical editors of the papers, to make the notices all the stronger and the better appreciated," coming as they did from persons who were "unbiased and naturally would feel it necessary to be as critical as possible."

In an article about Hazel entitled "A Remarkable Girl," the
Musical Courier admonished critics for their lack of perception in
referring to Hazel's "lack in artistic conception," and it cited her
youth and her courage in facing the critical Berlin audience:

It is a remarkable fact that the colored people, noted as a race for warm
emotional capacity and natural musical aptitude, should so far have
produced no artists of real worth. The Jubilee Singers doubtless were
endowed with voices of admirable quality and power, but their range of
songs was generally limited to simple negro melodies, affecting songs,
which did not, however, require the highest musical training in their interpretation. Whether the confusion of the reconstruction period or lack of
mental development, or both cooperating, have held their energies
dormant, still the fact remains that the cakewalk, the coon song and the
plantation hymn have been the musical province of the colored race. In
fact, we have never before known of a really artistic negro pianist or
violinist.

In view of this truth, the recent success of Hazelda Harrison, a young
colored girl of La Porte, Ind., is both interesting and significant. Like
many talented young women, Miss Harrison has fought her own way, for a
long time playing dance music until two in the morning in order to maintain
herself. It was at this time that Victor Heinze, the eminent Chicago pianist,
heard her play, and not only admitted her talent but offered her
instruction. That her schooling under him has been thoroughly good is
shown in her artistic playing, and expressly commended in Berlin
criticisms. In her recent appearance at Berlin Miss Harrison scored an
encouraging success. She was described by the critics as possessing
"smooth, flowing technic," "a decided feeling for tone beauty,"
"individuality," and "a beautiful piano tone." In fact the only adverse
criticisms upon her work were that her artistic conceptions were not fully
matured and that her *forte* was not sufficiently powerful.

Now, neither to the struggle of Miss Harrison's early life nor to her
present success does interest attach in the most overwhelming sensational
sense. Genius of all kinds has grown so addicted to hobnobbing with rats in
a garret that we feel no exciting thrills over a new story of plain persistence
and achievement. Moreover, Miss Harrison's triumphs may seem to be
somewhat qualified by the charge of "lack in artistic conception." When
we realize, however, that for this eighteen year old girl it must have been
more than trebly hard to face the metropolitan audience of Berlin, the most
critical in the world, and that thus hindered she has won what none of her
race has ever before attained, our surprise is far greater. This lack of which
the critics speak, moreover, is purely a matter of growth, broadening,
deepening, which must inevitably come with further study. Nothing but

commendation is expressed for her general artistic intuition and her surer technic. In other words, Miss Harrison has climbed the heights—now she must stop and absorb the soul uplift from the broader outlook before her. In the years to come she must work for an individual, more clearly marked, style in playing. Meanwhile she is deserving of high credit.[49]

Hazel's skin color made her an oddity in the Berlin of 1904. While for the most part it was her musicianship that was reviewed, two of the reviews were influenced by Hazel's own color. *Morgenpost* wrote:

Living in the time of the sensational, if not the musical wonder, we cannot pass a concert of a mulatto. . . . What she accomplished in rendering the Concerto in E Minor by Chopin and A Minor by Grieg was, I admit, not yet perfect in technic; it also lacked somewhat in tone development and physical power, yet we must acknowledge her musical intelligence and temper, her feeling for sounding beauty and a warmth of perception. In her rendition of Chopin's composition there was even a touch of poetry. Taken all in all, the little mulatto amounted to something of a sensation.[50]

An even more curious review had appeared in the *Musical Courier*:

This is the first time a colored girl has ever played in Berlin and the first time I ever heard a mulatto in serious composition in public. The concert was a success and a great surprise to most people in the audience. Miss Harrison is a very gifted girl. . . . She is a slight, comely girl of apparently seventeen or eighteen. That beautiful melancholy of the Chopin first movement was well brought out—perhaps because melancholy is a characteristic of the young woman's race. She is a pupil of Victor Heinze of Chicago, and she shows excellent schooling.

Her playing is really remarkable when one considers that the colored race has thus far done nothing worth mentioning in music. Our best negro songs are not the product of the black race, but of that white genius, Stephen C. Foster, and a freak like Blind Tom does not count, because he is not a musical nature, but simply a marvelous imitator. Hence, as Miss Harrison can claim to be the first colored person to attract the attention of the musical world as an artistic performer, she has accomplished much to be proud of. It certainly required great courage on her part to face an audience and the critics in this hotbed of music; but the results show that it was worth while. Is Miss Harrison a musical prophet arisen among the colored race, like Booker T. Washington, to show by her example what

others can do if they will try; or is it the Caucasian blood in her veins that is
doing the work, for she is not a full-blooded negress? At any rate, with the
race question becoming more and more a burning issue in the United
States, she stands out as an interesting and isolated case.[51]

While it is not known how Hazel responded to that critical tack,
she was probably not too surprised as such thinking was part and
parcel of the time. Nevertheless, the generally encouraging nature
of her reviews, with their comments on her artistic intuition, sure
technique, and the prediction of her further growth in breadth and
depth with the development of a more individual style, was
extremely heartening to her.

Hazel found life in Berlin very congenial. She and Birdie settled
in at 58 Steglitzerstrasse with a landlady who enjoyed preparing
good German meals for her guests. The next year, Portia Washington, Booker T's daughter, would live at the same address while she
studied music in Berlin.[52] During the morning Hazel and Birdie
worked on their German, and later in the day, they went for strolls
in the Tiergarten when Hazel was not practicing or away giving a
concert. Whenever possible, they attended concerts in the evening.
It was an idyllic time for them both.

Memories of Hazel's German appearance were still alive there a
year later. When Harriet Gibbs, director of music in the colored
public schools of Washingon, D.C. returned from Germany after
nine months of study, she reported that she had heard much in the
way of praise of Miss Hazel Harrison, who had made her debut at
eighteen with the Berlin Philharmonic Orchestra.[53] It is interesting
to see how Hazel's age at the time of the debut had come to be
reported as eighteen because the reviews had speculated that to be
her age. Over the years, the age at which she had appeared with the
Berlin Philharmonic gradually slid downward as far as it could
credibly go, and the spurious legend was established that she had
made that significant appearance at the age of twelve.

* * *

Hazel and Birdie returned to La Porte in January 1905[54] and
resumed the life that they had left in September. By 1907 Hazel had
some thirty pupils, most of them from prominent families of La
Porte and who had begun their study with her prior to her

departure. Their recital program for 1907 shows the wide range of proficiency of her pupils. The youngest and newest of them, Florence Low, was performing "Robin Red Breast Is Dead" and "The Cuckoo" after only a month's study. Florence Andrew, who had been studying with Hazel since age seven, was performing two intermediate pieces. Class-playing programs for 1909 and 1910 show Florence Low as having advanced to an intermediate pupil and Florence Andrew as playing more advanced piano pieces. By 1911 it had become necessary to have separate programs. The junior pupils—fifteen in all—gave their program in April 1911 to a large and attentive audience. The *Daily Herald* (8 April 1911) review noted that "the pupils all played well and the program was much more difficult this year than last year." Twenty-eight more advanced pupils were heard in recital on two consecutive evenings, June 19 and 20. The reviewer for the *Daily Herald* (20 April 1911) commented on how Florence Low surprised the audience with the perfect manner in which she played the "Tarantella" (Heller) and the "Valse Mignonne" (Thomas). "She did not make a single mistake and played in a brilliant way."

Although her pupils were progressing satisfactorily and their recitals reflected her competence and inspiration as a teacher, Hazel was paying a burdensome price in the toll her teaching took on her own practice time. Even though she lived at home and Birdie would not let her assume any household responsibilities, her teaching load still amounted to almost thirty hours a week. She continued to study with Heinze, traveling between La Porte and Chicago once a week. Practice time was somehow sandwiched in, most often in the late-evening and early-morning hours. Alone during these late hours, she was able to refine her musical perceptions and keep her personal goals firmly in view.

On February 6, 1910, Hazel gave a significant recital at Music Hall in Chicago. Reviewing it the next day in the *Chicago Tribune* (7 February 1910), eminent critic W. L. Hubbard wrote:

Hazel Harrison, a young negress who several seasons ago was brought forward in a series of recitals which showed that she was more than usually talented, reappeared yesterday in Music Hall. She was heard by an audience which filled the major portions of the concert room and which received her work with close attention and signs of hearty approval.

. . . The Chopin Sonata, op. 58 . . . sufficed to convince of the high quality of the young player's gifts. Her technic, always commendable, has gained in certainty, in fluence, and in brilliancy, and is now of a kind and degree which enables her to play with finish and authority such a work as the Chopin Sonata—a task by no means light. She gave a reading which showed not only that she had been intelligently and ably taught, but that she had gifts and talents of a distinctly musical character—gifts and talents which make unquestionable her more than usual aptitude for the career of a concert pianist.

Continuing, he wrote of Hazel's struggle:

It was learned upon inquiry that Miss Harrison has studied and is studying under the most difficult and trying conditions. Lack of financial means makes it necessary for her to labor at tasks which interfere with the technical development of her fingers, and her coming to the city for instruction is also accomplished only under the harshest conditions. It certainly would seem that a young woman so undeniably gifted and as sincere in her work as this one has proven herself to be should find the support and help of music lovers who have money to spare. There is so much money wasted upon instruction for young women who are devoid of talent that if a little of it could be devoted to the helping of this gifted one, who deserves well and will succeed, it would be a truly excellent thing. If narrowness of mind prevents some of our wealthy people from assisting, then some of the more fortunate of her own race should look to her helping. She will prove a credit to them if she be given the chance.

The same recital was reviewed by Glenn Dillard Gunn in the Chicago *Inter-Ocean* (7 February 1910), with comments on her technical proficiency: her fleet and strong fingers and clean and accurate execution of all merely mechanical problems. He felt, however,

that her pianistic mastery is still far from complete was evidenced by her very limited control of tone color. A singing tone she rarely produces and her manipulation of contrasts was not illuminative. This shortcoming was in part traceable to the Viennese school of piano playing of which her teacher is a prominent exponent. It is a school seldom distinguished by a lively sense of tonal beauty on the part of its disciples, who incline rather to nimbleness of finger and superficial brilliancy. In this sense Miss Harrison is typical of the school. A further pianistic limitation, and one that inevitably reacted on her command of tone, was revealed in Miss Harrison's too conservative use of the damper pedal. She habitually sacrificed the broad effect to clarity of detail.

Her interpretation of the sonata was, nevertheless, marked by good taste and much careful thought; most encouraging of all, by natural and spontaneous musical feeling. The scherzo was very charmingly done and the largo was even more convincing in its poetic feeling. A few years in Europe should advance Miss Harrison considerably in her art, chiefly because she will there not be handicapped by the racial prejudice. She is a negress—which closes many doors to her here.

Ten days later, on February 17, 1910, the *New York Age* reported a very encouraging response to the challenge in the *Tribune* review, with the announcement that two Chicago women, whose names were to be kept secret, had given $4,000 to Hazel Harrison for her anticipated return to Europe, "where she expects to play before royal personages." With the realization of her goal now within her grasp, Hazel finished out the year in La Porte. Her pupils had to complete their year's work, and she had numerous personal and musical details to attend to, chief among them her own admonition to "practice, practice!"

Finally, in September 1911, the word came in the form of a cablegram from the Hermann Wolff concert agency: COME TO BERLIN AT ONCE. LARGE TOUR ALREADY BOOKED. FIRST CONCERT IN BERLIN. The news was broken to La Porte in a front-page article in the *Daily Herald* on September 12:

MISS HAZEL HARRISON TO TOUR ABROAD

Talented Pianist to Leave This Month
to Appear in Concerts in European Countries

OTTO MEYER ALSO TO LEAVE LA PORTE

Grateful and Appreciative Friends to
Give Them Farewell Concert at Hall's
Theater Tuesday Evening. Mr. Meyer
Going West.

Miss Hazel Harrison, La Porte's talented and honored pianist, will leave soon for Europe, where she will go on a concert tour under the auspices of a large bureau. Otto Meyer, La Porte's brilliant violinist, will leave shortly for the West, where he will both teach and do concert work. Tuesday evening, September 19, the people of La Porte will pay tribute to both these artists at a farewell concert at Hall's Theater.

. . . Miss Harrison in an interview said that she expected to leave for Berlin the last of this month, the exact date being dependent on the rental of the family residence, 1306 Clay Street. "Mother will accompany me," she said, "although my mother will not remain with me. I have been called by Wolff's concert agency, though I guess Victor Heinze, my teacher, is behind it. Mr. Heinze is in Berlin. I shall study as well as do concert work in June, when the concert season is over. I regret leaving my many pupils but I will be back in a year and it is a chance of a lifetime which I have, one which I cannot miss."

La Porte is proud of its two artists and though all regret their departure, they are gratified at the additional honors which they will achieve while away. Their work will be watched and each laurel added will give much pleasure to the La Porte friends. Tuesday evening's concert will be a fitting expression of appreciation and a "God speed" to the two musicians by the people of La Porte. Miss Harrison appeared in concerts abroad some years ago so she is not entering new fields.

The relationship between La Porte and Hazel Harrison had always been one of mutual affection, and now La Porte was beside itself with pleasure at the recognition of her great talent. A farewell concert had been arranged to salute the town's two departing musicians, and the merchants decided to close their shops early on that evening. The *Daily Herald* (18 and 20 September 1911) carried a notice on page one of the early closings and printed the program for the occasion.

Since the farewell concert had been the big event in La Porte that evening, the next day's paper carried the story on the front page:

BRILLIANT CONCERT BY TWO ARTISTS

La Porte Pays Homage to the Genius of
Miss Hazel Harrison and Otto Meyer,
Both of Whom Will Soon Leave

A great ovation greeted Miss Hazel Harrison and Otto Meyer last night in their joint recital at Hall's theater, where musical La Porte was gathered to show their appreciation of these two artists and to bid them farewell, as Miss Harrison is going to Europe for a continental tour, and Mr. Meyer goes West on a tour. Both of these have gained much in tone and breadth of conception since their last appearance in this, their native city. A well balanced program greeted this enthusiastic audience, who showed their appreciation of this musical treat by according equal honors to these popular artists.

The first number on the program was a perfect little gem—a sonate from Haendel. Here the violin part by Otto Meyer and equally important piano part by his sister were given with perfect ensemble that will not soon be forgotten.

The Schumann Sonata and Chopin Scherzo were Miss Harrison's most musical numbers. In them she could rise above technique and give the audience a glimpse of the matured Hazel Harrison—the artist that realizes that music has much more to offer than pyrotechnic display and musical technique is merely a means to an end. Music, like human speech, must consist of something more than words. Deep thought and sympathetic expression are necessary to speak in words that command attention and linger in the memory. It is by these features in the rendering of the Schumann Sonata that Miss Harrison endeared and strengthened her position among music lovers of La Porte.

. . . The next numbers were two more technical impossibilities, the Oriental Fantasie by Balakirev and the Gruenfeld Tarantelle, played by Miss Harrison. In the former, one has first to master all technique—and then hide the same in a brilliant display of interpretation and expression. To such a one the piece is full of true musical worth. It is weird, of course—wonderful—so much so that only an artist can play it and a musician can understand it. The Tarantelle was in lighter vein, brilliant, and played with a fine sense of rhythm. Miss Harrison's efforts were appreciated, and after many recalls, she played a charming little Schubert Romance.

. . . In the closing group of piano selections Miss Harrison was . . . at her best. The first number, By the Sea, Smetana, was played with great finish and a most remarkable grasp of the composition as a whole. The brilliant waltz by Friml was not only played by Miss Harrison's unusual rhythm but with a dainty interpretation and delicate rendering that was indeed charming. As an encore Miss Harrison again held the audience spell bound by her usual brilliant rendition of Sakelinhoff's [sic] Dance of the Elfes.[55]

Very shortly afterward, Hazel and Birdie departed for Germany, with the intention of being gone for a year. Hazel had arranged for a friend—a Chicago pianist—to take her pupils. The Clay Street property had to be rented because Hiram was no longer in residence. Birdie was now committed to watching over the talent that she had so carefully nurtured, and Hazel happily accepted the arrangement.

2

THE GERMANY YEARS: 1911–1914

Berlin, 1911. What a fascinating world this must have been to Hazel! So many significant events were taking place in this great musical center. All around town were placards and programs with pictures of music dignitaries; covers of music journals featured artists in their best publicity poses. Efrem Zimbalist was to appear with the Philharmonic, and Richard Strauss's *Der Rosenkavalier* had its premiere. Emil Sauer and Ferruccio Busoni were hailed as "two titans of the piano." There was notice of the dedication of a new concert hall called the Simon Harmonium House, located at 35 Steglitzerstrasse. This hall, with a seating capacity of only 190, was designed for the presentation of small chamber music concerts and recitals.[1] Elsewhere, headlines revealed that John Philip Sousa and his band were on a world tour and that Leopold Stokowski was in Munich. There was also the exciting news that "Caruso is here!" The best seats cost $15, and people waited in line for as long as twenty-two hours in order to buy tickets.[2]

Other successful artists of the day were the operatic singers Amadeo Bassi and Alma Gluck. Vladimir de Pachmann had recently given a Carnegie Hall concert in New York; Arthur Friedheim, Russian pianist and pupil of Liszt, was performing widely. The names go on and on: Pasquale Amati, Carl Flesch, Rudolph Ganz, Ruggiero Leoncavallo, Ernestine Schumann-Heink, Joseph Lhevinne. From Vienna came the news that Arnold Schönberg, the "super-ultra modern composer, painter and poet," had gone to live in Berlin,[3] and that Theodor Leschetizsky was reported to be developing some new line of thought in connection with his works as composer and teacher.[4]

Aspiring young American musicians were attracted in great numbers to this hub of the musical world. Intent on European study, they were urged to contact the correspondents of the *Musical Courier* for information of the arrivals, concert appearances, vacation plans, and marriages of the Americans.[5] Having established itself as an official information center, the journal declared itself to be "the guide that has shown to our musicians the path to pursue in Europe."[6]

Among the Americans in Berlin that fall were three of Heinze's pupils at the Cosmopolitan School of Music and Dramatic Art in Chicago: Vida Llewellyn, Ruth Klauber, and Hazel Harrison.[7] Much was made of Vida Llewellyn's debut as a "pianist possessing many unusual attributes."[8] Ruth Klauber appeared with the Philharmonic under the leadership of Heinze, and it was duly noted. Very little notice was taken of Hazel's presence, aside from a brief mention in the *Musical Courier* that she would appear with the Berlin Philharmonic and concertize extensively.

By now, Heinze had become well known to the Berlin public, not only for the quality of his finished product, but also for the keen perception with which he selected masters under whom his students would complete their preparation. He had attracted considerable attention as an outstanding teacher, for during the 1911-1912 season, he had had five pupils make successful Berlin debuts. They had all demonstrated before the public to have been remarkably well grounded in the technique of piano playing.[9] In addition to the debutants, there were a number of other Americans studying with him in Berlin. So well regarded was Heinze there that he had decided to establish himself in Berlin and take advantage of his reputation, letting the Cosmopolitan School, of which he was director and head of the Piano Department, look after itself.[10] Establishing his studio at 35 Luitpoldstrasse, he advertised himself and prospered as "Victor Heinze, Pianist and Teacher. For many years exponent of Leschetizsky's principles of piano playing."[11]

Whether it was Victor Heinze or Hugo van Dalen, former Busoni pupil, who arranged for Hazel to play again for Busoni in Berlin is not clear from existing accounts. However, it is clear that she played for the great Italian master, and he recognized that the promise that was so evident earlier had indeed come to fruition. He said that she was gifted, had strength and poetry, and that if she would follow his advice, she would have undoubted success. Even though he had previously decided to take no more pupils, and had not done so for two years, he offered to direct her studies,[12] providing her with what today would be called a scholarship. He probably suspected that her resources were just adequate to see her through the year that she had planned to be there and that she would need assistance. Hazel and Birdie discussed the offer, and they decided that Hazel would remain for an additional year in Berlin to study with Busoni, and that, since there was no urgent reason for Birdie to return to La Porte, she, too, would remain in Berlin.

The opportunity that had been presented to Hazel—to study with the great Busoni—was a pianist's wildest dream come true. Ferruccio Busoni was one of the most eminent pianists of his time, playing to large and demonstrative audiences everywhere. His very name invoked awe and his musical presence was unforgettable. He was a musical superman who thought nothing of playing fourteen concerti in four programs or of programming the four Chopin ballades, six Liszt études, the two Liszt Legends, and the Don Juan Fantasy all on a single program.[13] It was said that there was nothing possible on the piano that he could not do without absolute mastery, and his command of the keyboard was nothing less than demonic.[14] From the limpid, graceful runs to the thundering technical display, there was an uncanny musical intelligence in command. Although Busoni had not studied with Liszt, or even heard him play, the kinship between the two was bound up with the art of piano playing. He was called the "reincarnation of the spirit of Liszt," and he carried the two Liszt Legends, "St. Francis's Sermon to the Birds" and "St. Francis Walking on the Waves," to the final goal of tone painting on the piano. Those who heard him play said that the listener actually felt himself to be wandering in the forest listening to the voices in the branches and hearing the gentle words of the saint speaking to the birds in tones they could understand.[15] Busoni, born in Italy, had lived in Moscow, Boston, and Weimar; in 1894 he had made Berlin his home, being one of the most distinguished of the city's many distinguished residents, and his energies there were spent giving recitals, composing, conducting, and teaching.

Hazel's becoming a pupil of Busoni was the second such for-tuitous circumstance in her life, when she came under the influence of the right person at the right time. The association with Busoni was a long and a close one, which she always cherished and which was central to her experience. As his pupil in Berlin, she had access to his home, his music, and hearing him practice. Busoni took charge of her broader education as well, giving her copies of the great philosophers to read and discussing them with her later.[16] His choices reflected his own philosophical direction, as he had been influenced at different times by Henrik Ibsen, Friedrich Nietzsche, and Gabriele d'Annunzio.[17] Hazel was always a welcome guest in the home of Gerda and Ferruccio Busoni, and it was there, where they often entertained students, that she heard good conversation and met many of the leading musicians of the time. Busoni's kind-ness toward his pupils and the hospitality of the Busoni home were as well known as were his musical gifts. Later, Hazel wrote, "The great ones have helped me—Busoni, Egon Petri, Bortkievitch [sic], Orth, Metcalf, Percy Grainger, and Harry Darling. I have studied with other great ones, but those mentioned are the Greats who have influenced my life."[18]

She failed to include Heinze on the list. Since his arrival in Berlin earlier that year and his subsequent decision to remain, he was doing well teaching the Americans—some of whom were promis-ing; others, less so. He had decided to make another important move: he would resume solo playing, and he firmed up plans to appear in Berlin, Munich, Breslau, Halle, and other music centers. There was the prediction that succeeding seasons would be as suc-cessful for him as the past one.[19]

But for so many others, success never came. While there was a great deal of news concerning the success of Americans and others, there were scores who were not successful. In Berlin alone, the actual number of debutant recitals in one season was approximately 600![20] There were certainly risks involved, and the unsuccessful stood to lose more than simply good reviews. It was not at all unusual for musicians who had gone to Europe for one or two years to return less well known than before they went. They did not get the engagements that they had hoped for, and their names disappeared from the professional world. Because their names did not make the bright lights, they were looked upon as failures, and the musical fraternities in their hometowns shunned them, since they were no different from any other group who likes a winner.[21]

The average student who went abroad could have done as well, if not better, by remaining at home—at least until he had learned all that it was possible to learn there before going to Europe. Berlin and other European cities were full of disappointed students. Many of them arrived unprepared musically and often financially, without any knowledge of the language of the country. For the musically prepared, there were many advantages to living in the atmosphere of the country where the languages of opera and lieder were spoken and sung.[22]

Instruction was as good in America as elsewhere; the European teacher was very often the American teacher who happened to be living in Europe and offered essentially the same training. The high-priced teachers, especially in Berlin, lived almost entirely on their income from American pupils. "Let the American crop fail for a few seasons," wrote *Musical Courier*, "and all of those instructors who get 5, 6, 7, and 10 marks a lesson would have to shut up shop. The Europeans simply will not pay these prices. . . . The sad feature of it is that so many learn nothing: they get no adequate return for money expended."[23] Heinze, riding the crest of this wave, was interested in its long life, and advertised thus:

VICTOR HEINZE   PIANIST AND TEACHER

Send for free booklet	Most modern principles
"Studying Music Abroad"	Thorough artistic education
	Eminently successful

European teachers possessed no marvelous method that a newcomer, often able to remain for only one season, would be able to grasp at once and return to America as a full-fledged artist. Additionally, it put the European teacher in the position of trying to accomplish the impossible, often undertaking work that he or she would rather refuse.

On the other hand, European study could be invaluable in preparing pupils who were really ready for further development and who had time and an adequate amount of money at their disposal. Hazel had certainly arrived at the stage where she was equal to the privilege of European study, and of study with Busoni. For the remainder of her career, her association with Busoni, and later Petri, would be her primary, door-opening credential. It was the way she was listed in the Howard University catalog: "Hazel Harrison, Instructor in Piano. Pupil of Busoni and Petri." That said everything.

In 1913 Busoni went to Bologna as director of the Liceo Rossini, and his pupils were taken over by his illustrious pupil and assistant, Egon Petri, who carried on Busoni's tradition in pianoforte playing. Hazel's musical life continued in essentially the same manner: studying, performing, reading, and attending concerts. But for the first time in her life—she was now thirty—there was a serious affair of the heart. The details are as sketchy as they are tantalizing: he was German, his family was very pleased with the match, and he had offered her a family heirloom ring to formalize an engagement. After some soul-searching, Hazel declined, her primary rationale being, "What would Birdie think?" and secondarily, "Perhaps I should marry one of my own." The decision haunted her for years. She almost never spoke of it afterward, but it was the big "What if—" of her life.[24]

1912. Jascha Heifetz, then eleven years old, created a sensation in Berlin.[25] The news came from Croydon, England, that Samuel Coleridge-Taylor was dead at thirty-seven. Wreaths and flowers were received from all the principal musical organizations of London.[26] Numerous professional musicians and friends were represented at the funeral, among them a South African delegation that brought an enormous wreath from its "African Black Brothers."[27] In Stuttgart, Richard Strauss's *Ariadne auf Naxos* received its premiere "before a brilliant international audience which recalled him ten times."[28]

1913. Stravinsky's latest ballet, *Le Sacre du Printemps*, was still being regularly hissed.[29] Cosima Wagner celebrated her seventy-fifth birthday.[30] Joseph Wieniawski died,[31] Wanda Landowska made her first appearance in Moscow.[32] and Paderewski appeared in Leipzig after an absence of many years.[33] Vida Llewellyn's star continued to rise, and notices from Dresden, Berlin, Breslau, and Halle declared her to be "an artist of superior order."[34]

The 1913-1914 season in Berlin had been a glorious one. The stellar operatic event had been the Royal Opera's production of *Parsifal*. Its staging was deemed to be every bit the equal of that of Bayreuth, and it was presented more than forty times in order to

meet the demand for seats. The solo instrumentalists appearing in
Berlin that season had included violinists Kreisler, Elman, Flesch,
Heifetz, Serato, Szigeti, and Enesco, and pianists d'Albert, Busoni,
Sauer, Rosenthal, Lhevinne, Dohnanyi, Petri, Gabrilowitsch, and
Schnabel. The vocal artists of the day were heard in great numbers
in concert and on the operatic stages; lieder were heard literally by
the hundreds. Oratorio societies drew large audiences; the Nikisch
Philharmonic concerts were invariably sold out; and the Royal
Orchestra concerts under the baton of Richard Strauss were sold
out a year in advance. The number of paid attendances by the
Berlin public to concert and operatic performances totalled
approximately 2,200,000. And that included only those events
playing to a large clientele; it did not include concerts with only a
fair degree of drawing power or less than full houses. Thus ended
the long, heady, golden afternoon of musical Germany.[35]

The war broke out in the summer of 1914. Life changed almost
immediately: theater halls were closed; music was not permitted in
the parks; and there was no dancing in the hotels. It was hard, at
the beginning, to realize what was happening, but as the word came
for Americans to leave, there was a deepening realization of its
seriousness.[36] Hundreds of people were stranded. Consuls organized
special trains to convey their citizens to Holland and then to
England. The trip was long and uncomfortable, with many inter-
ruptions. Often, only one piece of luggage was allowed. Gabrilowitsch had been arrested near Munich as a Russian spy and kept in
prison for fifteen hours. Later, he was taken to the Hotel Vier
Jahreszeiten under surveillance. He was able to get out of Germany
by way of Lindau and escape into Switzerland. Leopold Stokowski,
then a British citizen, was watched by the police and was finally
requested to leave, which he did, and he went to Holland.[37]

F. Wight Neumann, the impresario, relating his own experiences in an interview when he arrived in New York in September,
noted that the artists he was to manage in Chicago were safely out
of the war zone: Schumann-Heink, Zimbalist, Gluck, Bloomfield-
Zeisler, Gadski, Maggie Teyte, and others. He predicted that the
coming season in the United States would be a brilliant one and a
big money-maker.[38]

Hazel, Birdie, and the Kemper Harrelds, also in Germany, were caught in the turmoil. They were interned in Berlin for six weeks, after which the American government sent for its citizens, and they were permitted, through English intervention, to return to America. On the same ship were Alain Locke, Rhodes scholar and assistant professor at Howard University, and his mother. Because the English ship took care of British citizens first, others had to take places in steerage. It was under these extremely crowded and uncomfortable conditions that they returned to America.[39]

For Hazel, it was with reluctance, for Berlin had become home and German her language. Saying goodbye was painful; her sympathy for the suffering population was great. Not many had been prepared for this state of war and the experiences it brought: arrests, flights, harassment, and interrupted careers. The long idyll was over.

3

PREMIERE PIANISTE: 1914-1931

Hazel Harrison arrived in New York in September 1914 to find herself a celebrity. Immediately upon her arrival, Bishop and Mrs. Alexander Walters gave a reception for her at their home on West 134th Street. About seventy-five prominent guests were in attendance, primarily the musically elite of New York City. Mme. Maria Selika, the well-known prima donna and New York voice teacher, was among the guests, as were the organist Melville Charlton, Alain Locke, jazz pianist Luckey Roberts, bandleader and composer James Reese Europe, and J. Rosamond Johnson, just back from two years in London as director of Hammerstein's Opera House and now beginning his association with the Settlement School of Music in New York. An interesting program had been arranged, consisting of selections by the guest of honor as well as by some of the other talent in attendance.[1]

"Junkman's Rag"	Roberts
C. Luckey Roberts	
"Chaconne"	Bach-Busoni
Miss Harrison	
"Lil' Gal"	
"Since You Went Away"	
"Roll Dem Cotton Bales"	Johnson
J. Rosamond Johnson	
Trio (violin, piano, violin)	Bach
Miss Franklin, Miss Smith, Mr. Martin	
Song from "Valdo"	Freeman
William Freeman	

"In the Garden of My Heart"	Ball
Mrs. Freeman	
Group of waltzes	Chopin
Miss Elise Smith	
"Rag Time Sonata"	Roberts
C. Luckey Roberts	
"Adelaide"	Beethoven-Liszt
Miss Harrison	

While in New York, Hazel was stopping at the YWCA, then on West 132nd Street. Lucien White, whose column "In the Realm of Music" appeared regularly in the *New York Age*, wrote some six years later of the singular pleasure of hearing her play in that autumn of 1914. The recollection had been prompted by the announcement, in 1920, of her forthcoming New York appearance:

I heard Miss Harrison when she returned from Berlin, Germany, in September, 1914, but it was in a very private audience, only Kemper Harreld, myself, and one or two young ladies who were guests at the YWCA being present at the YWCA parlors. . . . She and Mr. and Mrs. Harreld were in Berlin at the same time and were fellow-passengers returning to America.

So out of friendship for her brother artist, she played for us. A student of the great Busoni, it was not surprising that she should have played the "Adelaide" by Beethoven, as transcribed by Liszt. Echoes of her playing that afternoon linger in my memory though six years have nearly passed. I am anxious to hear her again. If she has ripened and matured in accordance with the promise of that day she is truly to be considered a great artist.[2]

Continuing westward, Hazel first touched base in La Porte, with the promise to visit Chicago soon. Chicago regarded her as a near-native daughter, and the *Chicago Defender* chronicled her movements over a number of years.[3]

September 26, 1914

Miss Hazel Harrison, who has been abroad, is expected in the city to be the guest of Miss Elizabeth Clarke, 3812 Wabash Avenue.

October 3, 1914

MISS HAZEL HARRISON TO APPEAR IN CONCERT

World's Greatest Pianiste to Write for
Chicago Defender. Music Lovers Anxious
to Hear Her.

Chicagoans are glad to learn that Miss Hazel Harrison is back in
the States. It is likely that Mr. Cary B. Lewis will present her to
music lovers of this city in the near future. Miss Harrison, according
to the great masters abroad, is one of the world's greatest pianistes.
She has just returned from Berlin and is now at home in La Porte,
Indiana. Miss Harrison will write for the *Defender* some of her
experiences abroad and tell of her trip through the "war zone."
All Chicagoans are anxious to hear this noted and talented artist.

Back in La Porte, she had been engaged to play at a large concert
program on October 30, sponsored by the German Alliance for the
purpose of raising Red Cross funds. It was noted that she would
contribute one of the best numbers of her repertoire "and probably
will have to give more, as La Porte audiences never tire of the kind
of music she is able to give them."[4] However, since she was then
planning to give a recital, her decision to play at the benefit concert
was particularly appreciated. Other artists were also obtained for
the concert; of course, Hazel was the leading attraction. The *Chicago
Defender* continued to inform its readers of Hazel's activities:

October 17, 1914

COMING SOON

Miss Hazel Harrison, "world's greatest pianist," will appear in
recital soon. Watch for date. Biggest musical and social function of
the year. Miss Harrison has just returned from Berlin, Germany.

October 24, 1914

Miss Hazel Harrison and her mother were in the city this week,
the guests of Mr. and Mrs. Joe Brent, 3550 Prairie Avenue. Monday

evening they attended the Clarence White recital, and Tuesday
evening she was the guest of Mr. Carey B. Lewis at the
Assembly Dance.

The German Alliance benefit concert in La Porte turned out to
be a stellar event, primarily because it was the first opportunity for
the city to hear its talented daughter since she had departed three
years earlier, intending then to be away for only a year. The *Daily
Herald* (31 October 1914) reported the event with the enthusiasm
the concert must have deserved:

ART GALORE AT CONCERT OF ALLIANCE

Miss Hazel Harrison Shows the Town
Why Berlin Likes Her Piano Playing

With a program freighted with music illustrating the temperaments of
the Slav, the Teuton and the Latin, the German Alliance of La Porte last
night contributed its concert to aid the German Red Cross society. Madison
theater was crowded with an audience that expected the quintessence of art,
and had every reason to feel thus disposed. And the auditors were not
disappointed. It is to be doubted if a program containing a greater variety
of music, vocal and instrumental, of the very highest rank, ever was given
in this city.

The feature, of course, was the first public appearance after her years of
concertizing in Berlin, of Miss Hazel Harrison, who without exaggerating
the term, might now be called an eminent pianist. The fact that she was
able to gain a high mead of appreciation in the musical center of the world
must necessarily stamp her with possessing the skill that marks the
difference between the very good and the finest. Two superb interpretations of master compositions not only comprised a personal triumph for
herself, but created the indelible impression that this La Porte girl is a
credit to the city and is entitled to every mark of appreciation its people can
vouchsafe her.

. . . Miss Harrison tripped across the stage a smiling mass of femininity
and when arriving at the piano took up her task in the conventional artistic
way. The stool had to be just right, and when everything was adjusted *au
fait* her lithe fingers began with the Fantasia in F Minor, by Chopin.
Anyone who has ever played the piano sufficiently well to attempt the
works of the Polish master knows that to play Chopin faultlessly is about

the highest mark of ability. Besides, Chopin utilized the genus of the pianoforte better than any composer before his time or since, and this might explain more than anything else the popularity of his music with concert pianists.

With her own grand piano at her disposal, Miss Harrison brought out the beauties of Chopin in that artistic way that makes even the uninitiated musically to realize they are there. To make Chopin sound right it must be played well; and in this Miss Harrison unfolded the master's wonderful ideas after the fashion of pre-eminent interpreters. Every delicacy of tone, every contrast in touch, was at her fingers' ends. There was an agreeable absence of that smudge of tone that even good pianists are not free from cultivating. Each note was clear, incisive and gave its proper weight to the texture of the composition. Sonorousness in the lower strings was produced without the strenuous hammering that even many great pianists affect. And as the music flowed from the instrument, Miss Harrison sat before it a confident and keenly alert artist, glad of the opportunity to show the folks of her home town the reason why she likes to live in Berlin.

Miss Harrison carried away all the honors an enthusiastic audience could bestow. She is one of a very small class of pianists who has been able to so master her instrument that she seems to use it as her natural language. She has attained the position where technique is merged in art and forgotten. The listener only knows he is being led through a land entirely familiar to his guide, and there is nothing left to desire.

Applause that took on the nature of an ovation greeted her ears at the close of the selection. There was no getting out of an encore even had she wanted to, so she played another number by the same composer, in the same impressive way and with the same delightful effect. A bouquet of flowers was handed over the footlights by her admirers.

Appearing on the same program were a vocalist and a violinist. Accompanying the violinist was Ruth Mann, a former pupil of Hazel's. The review mentioned Ruth Mann's "remarkably able performance," which gained her general recognition that evening. Hazel must have been especially pleased.

November 7, 1914

The charming Miss Hazel Harrison of La Porte, Ind., was in the city this week on business. She paid a special visit to her friend, Miss Elizabeth Clark, 3812 Wabash Avenue.

The recital that Hazel had been preparing took place at the First Presbyterian Church under the auspices of the Amateur Musical Club. It was a program originally intended for a concert in Berlin, which, due to the outbreak of the war, did not take place. It turned out to be her American debut, and was attended by many friends from Chicago and South Bend. The Beethoven Sonata opus 57 ("Appassionata") opened the program, and "from the first touch of her nimble fingers upon the piano, with the deep chords of the melody, until the end of that stirring *non troppo* passage, the audience was spellbound." The *Daily Herald* review (10 November 1914) continued:

Technically speaking, her accent was faultless, and her phrasing was such as to weave one strain into the other, yet to punctuate it so as to make the melody more clearly understood. Perhaps the most marked virtue was the splendid balance of her hands, neither one being over trained. They seemed to work along in perfect harmony, which gave to her that even motion so much desired in passing from the lower to the upper register. Her use of the pedal is worthy of note. Most pianists have the idea that the use of the pedal is to either gain a forte or pianissimo tone color, yet to how much greater use did Miss Harrison put it. She accented with her pedal; she phrased with her pedal; in fact, she used it as another means by which she could bring forth that feeling which inspired her and which she wanted to give forth to her home people.

It seems almost a shame even to think of the practical side of piano study when one hears Miss Harrison, because her work is far above that. And "that" is the very thing which marks her as a genius. To be able to master the "common everyday things" in music, yet to still retain the musical idea after having gone through those months of practice and worry is the very thing for which every pianist strives.

The second number, the "Chaconne," by Bach, for violin alone, but arranged by F. B. Busoni for piano and concert work, was exceptionally well rendered. The arrangement is splendid and indeed a difficult thing, but Miss Harrison was equal to the occasion. She sang out the melody as if she were playing a violin, rather than as heavy an instrument as the piano. It is worthy of mention that Miss Harrison had the pleasure of playing it before Busoni.

Next came the "Adelaide and Busslied" by Beethoven-Liszt, showing how well she appreciates the lighter movements as well as the heavier. To this number she responded with "The Trout" by Schubert-Liszt, and "Liebesbotschaft" by the same composer, both being heartily applauded.

The next number, the "Valse de Concert on Motifs from Lucia and Parisina" by Liszt, was played by request. This composition is very difficult on account of the poem [*sic*] which it takes but again her sense of melody came into play and she never for one minute let the accompanying notes take precedence over that singing melody. To this number she responded with "At the Spring."

The last number, perhaps the most difficult of any on the program, the "Rhapsodie No. 12" by Liszt, was unusually well played. In this number she so held the audience that it sat perfectly quiet for several seconds after she had completed it, not knowing just what to do, to show their recognition of her wonderful work. Miss Harrison was so overwhelmed with the appreciation shown her by the people that all she could do was to come in carrying the two lovely bouquets of chrysanthemums, which had been presented to her during the evening, and bow in her own individual manner, making indeed a beautiful picture. Her debut to the public this year in the United States had been made and was truly a success.

Miss Harrison had planned on doing concert work this season in the South, but since the war people will not promise her any beneficial performances, so she has arranged for concerts in New York, Chicago, and Washington, but all are glad to say she will spend the intervening time at home.

Miss Harrison is a person of whom La Porte is indeed proud. It is with a feeling of one who is far above the average, and a spirit of great interest and Godspeed that all follow her as she goes into the world of music to make her fortune.

December 5, 1914 (*Chicago Defender*)

Miss Hazel Harrison of La Porte, Indiana, is expected in the city the last of the week to talk with her "press agent" about the advisability of having a big concert soon.

Hazel certainly bore the imprint of her famous teacher, not only in terms of her choice of repertoire, but in her dazzling technique as well. It was said of Busoni that if one had not heard him play during his peak, it was impossible to conceive of "the prophetic inspiration and grandeur of his performance. His technical achievements in mere speed and strength must have far surpassed anything accomplished by Liszt and Rubinstein." His span was huge; his "gradations of tone-color, perfectly controlled, and having the unbroken evenness of organ stops; a superb forte and fortissimo—it can be said unhestitatingly that the louder Busoni

played the more beautiful the sonority of his tone became."
Further, "he had a system of pedalling exclusively his own, by
which he would produce waves upon waves of resonance, through
which he could make a cantabile theme stand out in absolute
clarity."[5] References were frequently made to Hazel's pedalling,
whether, as in the above review, it was "worthy of note" or, as
someone said later, it was "sheer wizardry." Whether it was
intuitive or whether she had learned it from Busoni is a matter of
conjecture. But their artistic affinity made her the natural vehicle
for his expressive genius. In a sense, she became Busoni's American
presence. Her close friendship and her study with the master had
made her the instrument through which his ideas were personally
transmitted, and it was she who, in turn, transmitted them to
American students. Upon her return to the Chicago area, she gave
recitals for several music schools in the Loop for the benefit of the
advanced students who were studying some of the compositions by
Busoni, and for whom she could interpret as the composer had
instructed.[6]

The musical scene in Chicago and elsewhere was evolving toward
a greatly expanded level and volume of activity. Minstrel-type
shows were gradually disappearing, and in their place, a wider
variety of musical entertainment was appearing, accompanied by
supporting talent. Stock companies such as the Pekin and Lafayette
did an active business; choral groups enjoyed great popularity and
had good audiences; church choirs gave frequent concerts with
well-known soloists; and large "monster" concerts with choruses
of 200 and 300 voices attracted crowds of listeners.

The years after 1910 saw the rise of such artists as Clarence
Cameron White, violinist; Mme. E. Azalia Hackley, the "night-
ingale soprano of the race" whose mammoth Folk Song Festivals in
various cities did much to foster interest in Negro music; the
versatile Abbie Mitchell; and Florence Cole Talbert, Anita Patti
Brown, and Harry T. Burleigh, who achieved solid reputations as
singers. The Umbrian Glee Club in Chicago and the Clef Club in
New York were giving highly successful concerts.

Schools of music were established and flourishing. In New York
there were Will Marion Cook's Marion School of Vocal Music on
West 37th Street, with Harry T. Burleigh as voice instructor; the
Martin-Smith Music School; and the Settlement School of Music,
with J. Rosamond Johnson as an officer. In Chicago there was

Azalia Hackley's Normal Vocal Institute at 30th Street and
Calumet, which had as its aim the fitting of vocal teachers and the
training of voices for concert work, and, later, Pauline James Lee's
Chicago University School of Music was established.

Roland Hayes was beginning to delight large audiences, and in a
few more years, he would be an artist of unprecendented international acclaim. An unknown young woman from Philadelphia
would shortly sing before a meeting of the National Association of
Negro Musicians and astound them with her rare voice—launching
the career of Marian Anderson.

The winter of 1914 saw Will Marion Cook's Afro-American Folk
Singers in concert at Washington's Howard Theater. The group
included Harry Burleigh and Abbie Mitchell, "the race's sweetest
dramatic singer and soulful interpreter." The first all-colored
composers concert was given in Chicago's Orchestra Hall with
Mme. Anita Patti Brown, soprano, Chicago; W. Henry Hackney,
tenor, Chicago; R. Nathaniel Dett, composer and pianist, Hampton; chorus; and organ. It was given to encourage composers of the
race to let the public know that the Negro composer was a constant
contributor to the art of music.

The Umbrian Glee Club's sixth annual concert that year was an
evening with Afro-American composers: Burleigh, Lemonier, Will
Marion Cook, Coleridge-Taylor, and J. Rosamond Johnson. In
Symphony Hall in Boston on November 30, Mme. E. Azalia
Hackley presented the "grandest musical ever given in the east.
Soloists were Mr. R. Nathaniel Dett, Mr. Clarence White, with
quartettes, sextettes, and arrangements of soulful folk songs.'" A
short article in the *Chicago Defender*, December 5, 1914 noted:

SUNDAY AFTERNOON CONCERTS AT PEKIN

Sunday Afternoon Concerts with High Class
Artists To Be on the Boards at Once Famous
Playhouse—Hazel Harrison, Harry Burleigh,
St. Claire White and Madame Hackley to be stars.

With the beginning of the new year, the music lovers of Chicago will be
treated with the richest and grandest concerts ever heard in Chicago, is the
report from one who knows musically. It is said the real high class trained

artists will be engaged to give concerts on Sunday afternoons or evenings at the famous Pekin Theater. That such superb talent as Miss Hazel Harrison, Harry Burleigh, St. Claire White, Madame Azalia Hackley, Willie Tyler, Joseph Douglass, Patti Brown, Nathaniel Dett and others will appear in recital. [sic] It is believed that Chicago music lovers are just waiting for noted artists to appear and it will give hearty and liberal support to such a worthy artistic effort. Many clubs of the city have urged that such concerts be given in the "Windy City."

While the time may have been ripe for such concerts at the Pekin, not everyone was just waiting for those same artists to appear. Other kinds of entertainment still had a good audience:

DUDLEY AND MULE COMING

S. H. Dudley and his Mule are booked for the
Grand Theater. Coming soon. Biggest
vaudeville hit of the century.

Hazel's comings and goings remained newsworthy, and the *Defender* continued its coverage of her activities:

January 30, 1915

Miss Hazel Harrison of La Porte, Ind., will, accompanied by her mother, attend the Maude J. Roberts recital, Thursday evening, February 4 at Lincoln Center, Langley Avenue and Oakwood. . . . assisted by Cecil C. Cohen of Fisk and Oberlin.

February 12, 1915

Mme. E. Azalia Hackley is expected to be in the city in April. She and Miss Hazel Harrison may appear on the program at the Fortnightly recitals of the YMCA, of which Mr. Cary G. Lewis is manager.

February 20, 1915

La Porte, Ind., Feb. 19. It was revealed here today that Miss Hazel Harrison, the accomplished musician who has studied with Busoni in Berlin, Germany, will go to Chicago this week to make plans for a big recital in the spring.

Life was extremely busy for Hazel now. In addition to all the commuting back and forth between La Porte and Chicago, attending concerts, and appearing in musicales, she was trying to get her own concert career started. One of the cities she visited in 1915 and appeared in frequently thereafter was Atlanta. Her fellow Indianan and confidante from earlier Chicago and Berlin days, Kemper Harreld, was now director of music at Morehouse College. He saw to it that she appeared there before faculty and students as often as her schedule would permit. Furthermore, he was instrumental in arranging many concerts for her throughout the South. Hearing her play during one of those early visits was young Frederick Hall, then a preparatory student at Morehouse, who would later become one of her chief supporters when he went to Jackson College as director of music.

Hazel was often a guest in the Harreld household. She enjoyed the many gatherings there, with lots of good music and conversation, and the opportunity to practice while away from home. Harreld, a violinist, maintained a busy studio of violin and piano students. His young daughter, who had begun to study the violin, heard his piano students and repeated their lessons at the keyboard at every opportunity. Hazel recognized young Josephine's ability and encouraged her to study piano. Hazel and Harreld reached an agreement by which Hazel would teach Josephine whenever she was in Atlanta and he would carry out her instructions in her absence. This proxy arrangement, which "rescued Josephine from violin study," was unusual but not impossible, for she was a professional child and well versed in the discipline of study. Beyond study, Josephine's daily routine included hearing the finest music and being in close association with excellent musicians. "I can't recall when I first heard Hazel perform," says Josephine Harreld Love. "I grew up hearing her. It was a part of my daily life, and

Hazel was my best adult friend.''[8] This very close friendship flourished for many years to come.

Hazel had also resumed her teaching in La Porte and, at the same
time, was pursuing all possibilities for getting herself before the
public. She wrote to Alain Locke in 1915:

I am always teaching these days and studying German and practicing.
Really I think I have improved very much, am studying an ambitious
program for me. I played it in Chicago a few weeks ago at the Cosmopolitan School for the Ensemble class. Several critics were there and were
very kind. The next day I went to play to Mr. Gunn. He was also nice and
said I handled the piano in quite a different manner from the way I did
before I left.

I should have seen Mr. Busoni and missed him. However, he wrote me a
nice note. He expected me to come back after the concert and I was with
Birdie and she would not allow it because he hadn't left word at the Box
Office, and there he *had* all the time and was expecting me. I did not get it
till the next day. He had arranged that we meet at Mrs. Stock's the next
afternoon. You can imagine how distressed I was . . . I was so proud and
happy to think I knew him and of his beautiful kindness to me. He received
a regular ovation.[9]

Ever anxious to please, whether it was Locke or her audiences or
people who might be able to help her, she had to decline an invitation to play a concerto in Washington because she was to play for
"some very influential people in May and I want to spend all my
time on those pieces. . . . If it wasn't for the fact that I must play
very well for these people I would drop everything and study the
concerto, but I don't dare to now, so much depends on how I
please them."[10]

The Victrola had become a popular household item. The recording industry was beginning to boom, with boundless implications
for the future. Recordings by famous artists were popular
consumer items, but the industry had not yet included Negro artists
in their catalogs, except for jazz musicians and blues singers.
Notice of this omission appeared in the *Chicago Defender* (8
January 1916) as a brief comment in its "Around and About
Chicago":

It is unofficially reported that Miss Hazel Harrison and Miss Maude J.
Roberts will be asked to sing for the Edison people. If the readers of the

Chicago Defender in every city would call for records of these well known artists it would not be long before we would hear them, as we do Geraldine Farrar and Paderewski.

Elsewhere in the same issue of the *Defender* there appeared an article setting out forcefully the case for including Negro singers in the Edison and Victrola catalogs, noting that during the Christmas holidays, there were thousands of dollars spent by "our people" on Victrolas. A $250 Victrola for a Christmas present and seven or eight dollars for records were commonplace. These people were paying to hear Luisa Tetrazzini, Enrico Caruso, Mme. Schumann-Heink, Geraldine Farrar, and other noted artists. "But," the article asked, "how many of our race ever asked for a record of Mme. Anita Patti Brown, Mr. Roland Hayes, Miss Hazel Harrison, Miss Maude J. Roberts, Mr. Joseph Douglass? Are these not our great artists? Have they not been trained to the highest degree in their profession?" It noted that, while Bert Williams and the Fisk and Hampton Jubilee Singers were heard "in the Victrolas," the great Negro violinists or pianists were not. In asking what the reasons were, it answered the questions, perhaps naively, with the explanation that no demand was made. The article concluded, "Let the members of the race, when they go to Lyon & Healy and spend eight and ten dollars for records, call for our artists and be indignantly surprised because they do not have them."

By the end of the year, there had been no improvement in the situation, and the *Defender* again called the matter to the attention of its public, this time asking the recording companies why compositions by Negro composers were used in their machines but why individual artists were not represented. It noted that such compositions as "Jean" (Stantin-Burleigh), "Swing Along" (Will Marion Cook), "Who Knows?" (Paul Lawrence Dunbar-Ernest Ball), "When Malindy Sings" and "Banjo Song" (Dunbar) were Victor releases, as were such traditional titles as "Golden Slippers," "Great Camp Meeting," "Little David, Play on Your Harp," "Old Black Joe," and "Roll, Jordan, Roll." The Tuskegee Quartet was signing "Go Down Moses," "Good News," "Old Time Religion," and "Live a Humble." Still, individual artists such as Mme. Azalia Hackley, Mme. Daisy Tapley, Miss Hazel Harrison, Roland Hayes, Clarence Cameron White, and other celebrities were not included among the Victor offerings. The *Defender* called for readers to appeal to the Victor Record Company, asking that these noted artists be heard and saying that it would be profitable to have them as well as the numbers already included. The appeal closed by noting that the Victor people could be reached in either New York or Chicago, and that the matter should be attended to immediately.[11]

The plea fell on deaf ears, and several years passed before there was any significant recording of black concert artists. Among the first were Joseph Douglass, Roland Hayes, Marian Anderson, and Paul Robeson, who made his Victor debut in 1925 with a quartet of Negro spirituals. Once the ice was broken, the picture changed considerably, but the loss of those earlier artists to the listening public and to the recording industry was a sin of omission that can never be rectified, and the American musical scene is the poorer for it.

Hazel herself, though she continued as an active concert artist well into the 1950s, never made a commercial recording. Her initial reluctance may have been based on the primitive state of the art for so many years. Her views were no doubt colored by the views of her teacher, Busoni, who told of his own agonies when recording in the following letter to his wife:

My suffering over the toil of making gramophone records came to an end yesterday after playing for three and a half hours! I feel rather battered today, but it is over. . . . Here is an example of what happens. They wanted the *Faust* Waltz (which takes a good ten minutes), but *it was only to take four minutes.* That meant quickly cutting, patching, and improvising so that there should still be some sense left in it; watching the pedal (because it sounds bad); thinking of certain notes which had to be stronger or weaker to please this devilish machine; not letting oneself go for fear of inaccuracies; and being conscious the whole time that every note was going to be there for eternity; how can there be any question of inspiration, freedom, swing, or poetry? Enough that yesterday for nine pieces all of four minutes each (half an hour in all) I worked for three and a half hours.[12]

Nevertheless, Hazel was still at the peak of her powers when recording technology had been perfected. Offers were made and declined. Once, when a colleague asked her, "Miss Harrison, why don't you record just *one* something?" she replied, "Ohhh, I just can't stand the red light." And then she added, "You develop a nuance, and then some nincompoop will come in and turn a knob and make you crescendo when you didn't crescendo."[13] So she, in her own way, contributed to the lack of more widespread knowledge of her artistry. A few pirated tapes are in existence, but she would be the first to disown them. Many years later, in her final days, she made a tape recording—it was her idea—as a birthday present for her friend Reva Allman. As the final irony would have it, though, this treasured tape was taken on a picnic by Reva's daughter and erased by mistake.

Items from the *Chicago Defender* continued to document Hazel's movements. Her avid interest in the various social and cultural events of the day enabled her to meet many persons and to form many friendships that were to influence greatly her life and career in later years.

January 8, 1916

Miss Hazel Harrison, La Porte, Ind., was in the city last week and was the guest of the Brents on Prairie Avenue. Mr. Walter Anderson made it very pleasant for the visitor.

July 22, 1916

Miss Hazel Harrison, La Porte, Ind., was in the city last week. She was given an auto drive to Evanston, Ill., and a dinner party by Mr. Walter Anderson. In the party were Miss Elizabeth Clark and Cary B. Lewis.

July 29, 1916

Miss Elizabeth Clark and Mr. Walter Anderson were guests of Miss Hazel Harrison, La Porte, Ind., Sunday. Mr. Anderson motored in his Overland.

August 26, 1916

Miss Hazel Harrison, La Porte, Ind., passed through the city this week en route to Baldwin, Michigan. Upon her return she will be the guest of Miss Elizabeth Clark, 3812 Wabash Avenue.

January 6, 1917

Miss Hazel Harrison, La Porte, Ind., was in the city last week and stopped with Mr. and Mrs. Joe Brent, 3550 Prairie Avenue. She was entertained at dinner Wednesday by Miss Bertha Moseley and a theater party was given her by Miss Elizabeth Clark. Miss Harrison expects to give a recital in the early spring.

January 20, 1917

Miss Hazel Harrison, La Porte, Ind., will attend the recital of J. Rosamond Johnson at Institutional Church.

February 10, 1917

Miss Hazel Harrison, La Porte, Ind., is expected in the city Monday Feb. 19 to attend the Assembly dance and charity ball.

March 10, 1917

Miss Hazel Harrison, La Porte, Ind., will be in the city Wednesday to attend the recital of Maude J. Roberts, Wednesday, March 14, Lincoln Center. . . . Roy Wilfred Tibbs, bachelor of music, will assist Miss Roberts.

September 1, 1917

Miss Hazel Harrison, La Porte, Ind., who has been at her summer cottage at Idlewild, Michigan, arrived in the city Tuesday with her mother and is the guest of Miss Bertha Moseley, 6248 Sangamon St.

November 17, 1917

NOTED PIANIST HERE MONDAY

Miss Hazel Harrison, La Porte, Ind., noted pianiste, who spent several years at study in Germany, was in the city Monday evening attending Miss Moseley, 6248 Sangamon St., who is improving.

February 16, 1918

MISS HAZEL HARRISON TO GIVE RECITAL

Miss Hazel Harrison, pianist of rare ability, and one who has had the good fortune to study abroad, will spend a few days in the city as the guest of Mrs. Cary B. Lewis (nee Moseley), one of her chums, prior to her recital, which will be under the management of Julius N. Avendorph.

February 23, 1918

Miss Hazel Harrison of La Porte, Ind., the world's greatest colored pianist, will make her first appearance before her own people on Monday evening, April 18, at the South Park Church, 33rd and South Park Avenue, under the management of Julius N. Avendorph and Frank B. Waring.

May 11, 1918

PIANIST AND MOTHER VISIT CITY

Miss Hazel Harrison, La Porte, Ind., and mother were in the city Sunday and Monday and stopped with Mrs. Henrietta Wilson, 3533 Wabash Avenue. Miss Harrison attended the Lafayette Players and heard Mme. Daisy Tapley and Mme. Florence Cole Talbert in concert at Quinn Chapel Tuesday night. Monday she was the guest of Mrs. Cary B. Lewis, 6248 Sangamon St. Miss Harrison has been abroad studying music.

November 1919 saw Hazel in recital at Kimball Hall, Chicago, under the management of F. Wight Neumann, the noted impresario. The list of celebrities whom he managed included Geraldine Farrar, Sergei Prokofiev, Fritz Kreisler, Leopold Godowsky, Sergei Rachmaninoff, Percy Grainger, Enrico Caruso, and Pablo Casals. Reviewing the recital for the *Chicago American*, Herman DeVries hailed Mr. Neumann as "the Abraham Lincoln of musical impresari . . . who has let the sound of falling shackles accompany his gift of opportunity to a woman whose talents are certainly more to be considered than the hue of her skin."

Regarding her playing, he noted that she had "unquestionably exceptional talent . . . [and] gave able account of herself as an artist of extraordinary musical intelligence. Perhaps her greatest appeal lies in the sympathy of her tone, although her technique is well nigh perfect." In one of the most memorable phrases ever written about Hazel, he said, "But it is her heart that plays. Her fingers are but the obedient medium." He concluded by noting that the large audience plainly understood that it was in the presence of a real artist, and the recalls for Miss Harrison were numerous.[14]

It was the fashion of the day for black artists to try to enhance their prestige by referring to themselves as "Bronze Melba" or "Black Patti" or "Yellow Tetrazzini." Hazel never lapsed into that. She insisted on being Hazel Harrison, pianiste, standing on her own artistic merits and winning acclaim on that basis. Nor did she take the other route—that of being an exotic, of adopting the name and mannerisms of a Spanish or Latin American artist. One reviewer, admitting of the obstacles in Hazel's way, frankly suggested that she might do so. Henriette Weber, music editor on the *Chicago Examiner*, said of her:

Hazel Harrison is a young pianist with a real gift for the keyboard. Her playing is musical, mature, and individual. Extremely talented, it seems too bad that the fact that she is a Negress may limit her future plans. She is comely, and if a clever agent could put her forward under a name with a Spanish flair, a big future would be open before her. As it was, she attracted a capacity audience to Kimball Hall.[15]

It was no less than Glenn Dillard Gunn who offered to get her on the vaudeville stage, under an assumed name. She wrote to Alain Locke:

He would get someone to arrange the whole thing. He said the way I played I should have at least four or five thousand dollars to pay for extensive advertising and I would never earn it giving concerts as Hazel Harrison. What the American public wanted was something foreign and that I would succeed in this way. At first I could not stand the idea. It seemed so utterly impossible. Another thing—why is he so keen about it? Of course, I suppose I would earn money, but then do you think one can do *anything* for money? He also argued that the dignity of the vaudeville stage had been raised by such artists as Carolina White, Schumann-Heink . . . appearing. But they had made their names before. Once one is famous and then one can do most anything, don't you think?[16]

There were other problems, too. While Mme. Azalia Hackley's fifteen rules for colored women artists, published in the *New York Age*, may have been somewhat removed from the kind of life Hazel led on the road, they were not entirely removed, and they offer an interesting picture of the times:[17]

Hints to Young Colored Artists

By Mme. E. Azalia Hackley

Fifteen Rules for Women Artists

1. Don't pay more attention to the men folk than you do the women (at least until you get the women for friends).

2. Don't fail to keep close to the heels of your hostess. She will protect your good name.

3. Don't get angry and lecture the audience because they laugh at the wrong place.

4. Don't scold an accompanist before an audience, and be careful of the adjectives that you apply to her or her work behind her back. In a day or so she cannot be expected to do justice to music that it has taken you years to learn. Then, too, not all pianists have the knack of accompanying.

5. Don't brag about what you are artistically and socially. It is the surest way to cause doubt and inquiry into your record.

6. Don't entertain men while you are in bed. It is vulgar and injures the chances of those who follow. It is not fair and square to the profession.

7. Don't ride around in buggies or cabs with men just to have a good time. It is not fair and square to the profession.

8. Don't play cards, drink, or dance in a town while making money from a church which is against these things. It is not fair and square to those that give you money.

9. Don't speak of your audience as ignorant and uneducated and still take their money. It is not fair and square. Suppose they should inquire if you have any college diplomas hanging on your walls.

10. Don't come strolling in a house or colored boarding school at one or two in the morning and think you are privileged. It is a bad example to children, students, and local aspirants.

11. Don't accept invitations from the husband of your hostess without her knowledge. (She may ask you to remove your trunk.)

12. Don't believe that men are in love with you because they rave over your work or you. The more effervescent men are the quicker they become "dead" lovers.

13. Don't run away from the friends who have given you money and hospitality just to evade riding in a "Jim Crow" car. It is not fair and square. Ask the friends to help you. They will move heaven and earth to assist you.

14. Don't stop at hotels. Insist upon being with a family. All public people are liable to be misunderstood and talked about. It pays to be in a home.

15. Don't be dissatisfied with the boarding place provided for you unless

the people are bad or exceptionally untidy. Plenty of nice people are untidy. Don't eat if the things do not look right. Plead illness. The loss of one or two meals will not hurt.

Early in 1920, Hazel, now thirty-seven, moved to Chicago to be more conveniently situated for the demands of her career. She moved into 3745 Prairie Avenue with Birdie, two grand pianos, and Walter Anderson. The marriage to this handsome and charming man had taken place in the summer of 1918. Her letters now bore the proud signature "Hazel Harrison Anderson," and there was always the fond closing, "Birdie and Walter send love." Life continued for her, however, pretty much as it always had. She continued to give lessons in La Porte, but this would be her last year. She maintained her demanding practice schedule and her concert appearances.

The role of marriage in her life was secondary, very secondary. Although the marriage lasted for eleven years, Hazel was never inclined to be housewifely and had no inkling of, nor interest in, running a household. Birdie would cover for her as best she could, but Birdie's relationship with Walter was a stormy one, and she often put him out of the house for days at a time. Hazel did not seem to mind. He would return, and the word would circulate around Chicago, once more, "Walter's back!"[18] It was clear to many that Walter was, apparently, a rolling stone. Hazel's letters to friends would mention that Walter was in the real estate business, or that "I think Walter will go to New York," or "Birdie and Walter are well. The latter is going into the cosmetic business," and finally, "Walter is returning to real estate!" No one was surprised when the marriage ended in divorce in 1929 and Hazel's maiden name was restored by the court.

During this last year of teaching, Hazel went to La Porte by train every Saturday morning, giving lessons all day at the home of Dr. Fargher, whose older daughters were her pupils, and returning to Chicago in the evening. Louise Fargher recalled that, although she was too young at the time to take lessons, she would sit on the stairs in her house and listen. Once, she became so enthralled that she lost her balance and fell over the bannister. In recalling Hazel's delightful sense of humor and the extreme admiration in which her pupils held her, Louise Fargher remembered a dress that she, Louise, had with four pockets, which Hazel would always fill with

peanuts when she came.[19] Hazel's love for peanuts and her belief in
their salutary value later became another part of the Hazel legend,
and many a latter-day pupil remembers that when a lesson was
going badly, she would excuse him or her, saying, "Baby, go get
yourself some peanuts and get yourself together!"

In May 1920 Hazel appeared in Rankin Chapel at Howard
University. Of this concert, the reviewer noted that Miss Harrison
was perhaps the leading pianiste of the race, and he proceeded to
list the pieces she played: the Bach-Busoni "Chaconne," a scherzo
and a nocturne by Chopin, and several other compositions. He
admitted that they were all played with abundant feeling and
faultless technique, but he closed with the wistful statement that
"one or two lighter compositions would have lent variety to the
program."[20]

All of Hazel's programs reflected the influence of the mighty
Busoni, who epitomized the great German tradition of pianism that
had begun with Liszt. Hazel was solidly in that tradition. Her programming was weighted toward the technically difficult and
demanding Liszt tone poems and the Busoni transcriptions of Bach
and Liszt. The Liszt B Minor Sonata was a special favorite of hers.
And she was physically equipped for the demands made upon her
by this repertoire. Seeing her on the concert stage in a sleeveless
gown, one could watch her arm and back muscles undulate as they
met the demands she placed upon them. Many of these heroic
works, which she so favored for her concert programs, as did her
teacher, are rarely heard today ("St. Francis Walking on the
Waves," for example), as these grand pieces belonged to her and to
another era.

The 1920s saw Hazel well established as a concert pianist, her
reputation solidly secured, and with a busy schedule of concert
appearances. Many of her engagements were in smaller towns,
where her appearance might be under the auspices of a music club,
church, or social center. The recital would most often take place in
a church or high-school auditorium. Rarely would there be a piano
in top condition, but she somehow, instinctively, turned poor
conditions into a memorable musical experience.

During this decade, as well as the two that followed, rigid
patterns of segregation prevailed over much of the land. Outside of
the Phyllis Wheatley YWCAs in the larger cities and a possible
hotel here and there, public overnight accommodations were not

available. It was more likely that she would stay with a prominent local citizen—the doctor or minister or high-school principal. During appearances on college campuses, she was welcomed to the home of the president. Travel from one performance to another was by train, and in the South, where so many of her engagements were, that usually meant getting there by Jim Crow coach. Recounting one train ride into West Virginia, Hazel wrote to Alain Locke in June 1920:

This is my second day home, and I haven't been able to settle myself to anything. I think I am tired mentally and physically. Then too it is extremely hot, but Monday, I must start in practicing. Well, the ride to Charleston was uneventful. When we came to the border of West Virginia they took down the sign "colored" and I was no longer a thing apart, but an ordinary human being and the white people entered and there was no prejudice!! Then there was the wonderful scenery . . . the most inspiring sight to me because Chicago and environs are perfectly level. There had been heavy rains for two days and the heavy stones and dirt had rolled on the track. They called it a slide, and that delayed me some time.

Arrived at Charleston about six o'clock the next evening instead of 11:30 the next morning. Rev. [Mordecai] Johnson arranged for me to stop with Mrs. Fannie Cobb Carter . . . Rev. Johnson secured a Steinway from a friend and I practiced at the church about an hour, then the tuner came and I returned to the Carters and before I knew it it was time to return. Mrs. Carter had filled my Washington basket with roses and the church was nicely decorated. About 800 people were there—so many white people. About one-sixth. They were very enthusiastic. Many recalls. I am so glad. I did so want to please them.[21]

In West Virginia she was intrigued by her glimpse into another way of life in the "wonderful mountains," making note of the Carters' Jersey cow,

complete garden and everything that makes country life pleasant . . . electricity and plenty of hot water and a motor and all of the conveniences of city life. Mr. Carter is a lawyer. He is a wonderful man. Gets up every morning between 4 and 5 and works this garden and it feeds them summer and winter, and pays the taxes on itself. . . . They are thrifty like the Germans.[22]

The next day was a day for sight-seeing. Her hosts made certain that she saw all the important sights that related to her people.

They visited Booker T. Washington's birthplace in nearby Malden, West Virginia, and they proudly pointed out the businesses that were owned or managed by colored people, "not at all segregated." They visited a bank, meeting a friend of Locke's, who "was so nice and said nice things of my playing." She was especially interested to meet "Mr. James, the owner of the town's wholesale grocery and produce company. He is the only one of the colored race in the U.S. engaged in this business. A member of the Chamber of Commerce of Charleston."[23] Perhaps she was identifying with another "only black—only colored—only mulatto" as she listed his accomplishments. In closing the letter, she extended, as always, a welcome to Dr. Locke and his mother to visit her and Birdie in Chicago and referred again to his "beautiful kindness" on the long and difficult trip back home after the outbreak of World War I.

Black colleges, more removed from the cultural mainstream, were anxious to provide first-rate cultural enrichment for their students. Many students were from towns in which exposure had been limited at best or from rural areas in which there had been none at all. Artists were on the move during this time, singly and in groups, and it was not at all unusual to read in the newspaper that Ted Shawn, Ruth St. Denis, and the Denishawn Dancers had performed at Hampton, or that Nathaniel Dett had appeared at Shaw University, or that Florence Cole Talbert had been royally received on her tour of southern colleges. Once, when Hazel returned from "some very interesting concerts in the south," she wrote that "Mr. R. Hayes and accompanist had preceded me. They had even been to Paducah, Ky. and Evanti at Alabama State and Miles College out from Birmingham."[24]

When Frederick Hall went to Jackson College, Mississippi, in the early 1920s, one of his first thoughts was to bring Hazel Harrison to Jackson to give a concert. Her first appearance there was sponsored by a fine arts club and took place at Farish Street Baptist Church, where she was received with great enthusiasm. Her subsequent appearances in Jackson were at the college, and she sometimes remained for several days, giving workshops. Dr. Hall, for whom the college later named its new music center, recounts that after one of Hazel's Jackson College recitals, the manager of a local business telephoned the college to see if she would have the time to give a recital downtown, "at the store, so that our people can hear this very fine artist.'' Arrangements were made for a piano, and provision was made for her to play for the people the company invited. Dr. Hall remembers that it was a large and integrated audience and a very successful concert.[25] But not all Mississippi music lovers were yet free enough to grant total recognition to a Negro artist. The reviewer for the *Jackson Daily Clarion* noted:

Some of the prominent musicians of the city were delighted at an informal recital given by one of American's greatest piano artists. Her name is Hazel Harrison and she is a mulatto, but she is also an artist of the very highest order. Lovers of music and of real artistry in piano playing forgot that she was a mulatto and heard only the divine chords that flowed from her fingers.[26]

During his stay at Jackson College, Dr. Hall subtly crusaded against many of the indignities of segregation and developed in his students a perfection of performance that counteracted efforts from other quarters to convince them of their inferiority. In 1926 he left Jackson to return to Atlanta as director of music at Clark and Morris Brown colleges. As often as possible, he would join with Kemper Harreld to have Hazel Harrison perform in Atlanta, where she was by now a regular with a substantial following.

In July 1920 the National Association of Negro Musicians met in New York, their first meeting since their organization the year before. The publicity for the meeting announced that Hazel Harrison would play at the opening-night concert. This was to be her first public appearance in New York, and there was to be no admission fee to the recital. But she did not appear, and the reasons why were never really clear. The *New York Age* suggested that if the Program Committee named her for that duty without her knowledge or consent, she was certainly owed an apology; on the other hand, she may have accepted and then failed to schedule the appearance, in which case, both she and the committee were singularly embarrassed.[27] Many years later, in 1949, they did manage to get their dates together. She played in the Hollywood Bowl with the Hollywood Bowl Symphony Orchestra at the association's twenty-sixth convention, an appearance that she regarded as one of the highlights of her career.

On October 26, 1920, Hazel opened her recital season in Detroit under the management of the Aeolian Concert Bureau. In November she made another appearance at Kimball Hall in Chicago. Nora Douglas Holt's review was a high-water mark of critical acclaim:

After the recital of Hazel Harrison, pianiste, at Kimball Hall Friday evening, but one logical opinion could be deduced: that she is the last word in musical artistry and belongs in the galaxy of premier virtuosos of today. Her magnificent playing combined the technique of Godowsky, the toneism of de Pachmann, the romanticism of Hofmann, the architecture of Bauer, the power of Busoni, and the imagination of Paderewski.

The Toccata for Organ in C Major by Bach, and arranged by Busoni, the Fantasie quasi Sonato [sic] by Liszt, and the Islamey by Balakirev were the highlights of the program, while the "Governess" scherzo by Chopin was made a thing so vital that Miss Harrison, too, was caught in the flow of enthusiasm.

She played as one inspired and the audience returned her magnetic waves of musical thought by their eager and earnest applause.[28]

More and more, the musically knowledgeable were insisting on Hazel Harrison's absolute eligibility in the front rank of U.S. artists. This crusade also pushed for the inclusion of other equally qualified black artists, and the black press joined in urging such recognition. The *New York Age* of December 4, 1920, proclaimed

HAZEL HARRISON IN RANKS OF THE WORLD'S GREATEST ARTISTS

When modern composers are spoken of, Harry T. Burleigh's name is always one of the first mentioned. There is no color bar in his case. His voice gained recognition for him years ago and placed him as soloist in some of the largest and wealthiest churches of New York City—one an Episcopal congregation and the other a Hebrew Synagogue. On the concert stage he has appeared in the finest auditoriums in the country before the most cultured and exclusive audiences. His compositions are on the programs of the greatest artists, not just now and then, but as frequently as they appear in recital. And his knowledge and musical culture have placed him as a music editor with one of the most prominent publishing firms in the world—G. Ricordi and Company.

Augustus Lawson of Hartford, Connecticut, a product of Fisk University, is referred to, not as a Negro, but as one of the country's six greatest pianists. His ability has wiped out the color line.

Melville W. Charlton of Brooklyn is a colored man, but he is never considered as a "Negro organist." On the contrary, he has for years presided at the organ of a great Hebrew Synagogue and has given organ recitals in all sections of the country. He has occupied the conductor's desk in operatic recitals on any number of occasions and as teacher and accompanist he finds practically all of his time occupied. He takes high rank as a composer. And he is an Associate of the American Guild of Organists. The color line does not exist when Mr. Charlton's ability as a musician is under consideration.

Roland Hayes—in England now—is being received as an artist on his merits, as was Samuel Coleridge-Taylor in his day. The list could be continued indefinitely.

As a matter of fact, all of the above has been written as an introduction to the subject of Hazel Harrison, PIANISTE. Hazel Harrison is a colored girl and she has advanced to the first rank in the profession of music with the pianoforte as her instrument of expression. Industrious and sincere application, steady and unremitting practice, and assiduous devotion to an ideal has [sic] elevated her now to a plane where the color line does not exist. In America and in Germany her study and application led to one end—the highest possible development of her talent and her genius. And recompense for all the sacrifices made, for the hard tasks overcome, is found in the recognition accorded her by virtue of her attainment.

F. Wight Neumann is an *impresario* with offices in Kimball Hall, Chicago, and for thirty-four seasons he has been presenting to audiences in the Windy City the greatest exponents of musical art the world has produced. For instance, the season of 1920-1921 was opened by Enrico Caruso, the world's greatest tenor. Caruso was followed by Geraldine Farrar, soprano, of the Metropolitan Opera Company, Leopold Godowsky, Ossip Gabrilowitsch and Harold Bauer, pianists, and Fritz Kreisler, violinist. Comment on those names is superfluous.

Then came Hazel Harrison, who was not billed as a great Negro, but simply as a *Pianiste*. The 64-page prospectus issued by Wight Neumann, announcing his artists for 1920-1921, carried Hazel Harrison's photo in juxtaposition to Sergei Rachmaninoff, the composer-pianist, whose C-sharp minor prelude has made his name a household word and whose recital followed two days after Miss Harrison's. Other world famous musicians appearing this season are and will be Rudolph Ganz, Josef Lhevinne, Pablo Casals, Guimar Novaes (the young Brazilian pianiste), Percy Grainger, Jacques Thibaud, and many others.

Needless to say, Miss Harrison was not placed by Wight Neumann as a regular artist in his recital series because of her color. Nor did color prevent recognition of her ability as an artist.

Her large public followed her concert engagements through the *Defender's* coverage:

April 9, 1921

Kemper Harreld of Atlanta, Georgia, presented Hazel Harrison, eminent pianist, in recital at the First Congregational Church of that city, Tuesday evening, April 5.

June 11, 1921

Many of the local musicians who have been touring during the winter are back in Chicago and all report interesting trips, artistically and financially. Some of those who have recently returned are Hazel Harrison, pianist. . . .

September 24, 1921

Hazel Harrison, Patti Brown, and others are arranging their winter dates.

October 29, 1921

Hazel Harrison is on an extensive tour which will keep her out of the city until Christmas. She has recently appeared in Springfield, St. Louis, Kansas City, Wichita, and has engagements in Texas and New Orleans. Her programs reveal the same lofty purpose of giving her audiences high class music. Program notes assist hearers to better appreciate the compositions.

April 29, 1922 (*New York Age*)
HAZEL HARRISON
In Recital May 5th
Special Music Week

Jackson School of Composition and Music, E. Aldama Jackson, Director, takes pleasure in announcing the first appearance of Miss Hazel Harrison, premier pianist of our race, in recital at Aeolian Hall, Friday evening, May 5.

As Miss Harrison has many friends here among both races who have not heard her since her return from abroad, great interest is being evinced in her coming appearance.

All pianists, students, musicians, and lovers of music will surely be on hand to greet her.

After the May 5 concert at Aeolian Hall, Lucien White of the *New York Age* (13 May 1922) lamented:

Ninety-nine and nine-tenths of New York's alleged music lovers and devotees of culture were absent, but the one-tenth of one percent who were present enjoyed such a musical treat as has not been set forth in New York within the memory of this reviewer. And there was sincere warmth and fervor in the appreciation shown for the artist's playing.

She played the following program:

Choralvorspiel	Bach-Busoni
"In Thee Is Joy"	
"I Call Thee, God"	
"Now Rejoice, Dear Christian"	
Sonata in the form of a Fantasie	Liszt
(after a lecture on Dante)	
"Maiden's Wish"	Chopin-Liszt
Nocturne ("My Joy")	Chopin-Liszt
Scherzo	Chopin
Concert Etude ("By the Sea")	Smetana
"Danse des Elfes"	Sapelnikov

"Confessonal Song"	Beethoven-Liszt
"At the Spring"	Liszt
"La Chasse"	Paganini-Liszt
Concert Valse on Two Motifs (from "Lucia" and "Parisini")	Donizetti-Liszt

White's review continued, calling attention to the fact that

the race has produced some notable pianists, but it is no reflection upon their achievements to say that Hazel Harrison is in a class by herself, and that a class at the head of all the others. From sounding the first notes of Bach's Choralvorspiel—a trilogy of chorals transcribed by Busoni, with whom Miss Harrison studied—to the end of the long program, the pianist demonstrated her mastery of the art and science of piano playing. The most taxing demands upon her technique were met with an ease that approximated nonchalance; the most intricate harmonic figuration was given with a clarity and clear-cut definiteness that brought out each note as the master craftsman brings out the beauty of each jewel set in its frame of gold.

The Bach Chorals were given with dignity and classic severity and afforded a striking constrast to the Liszt Sonata, immediately following. The Chopin numbers were full of delicacy and ethereal lightness and their charms were fully developed by the pianist. The Smetana Etude, the Sapellnikoff Danse des Elfes and the Beethoven Confessional Song were played in a manner that brought out all of their contrasting moods. The last named, specially, is a composition of beautiful design and structure, and Miss Harrison gave it a most sympathetic interpretation.

The last three numbers on the program afforded wide scope to the artist's ability. Tremendous technical difficulties were in evidence, but were negligible by reason of the pianist's developed equipment. Delicate nuances followed lovely tone shading and passages filled with dynamic contrasts—melodies of soft sweetness, harmonies of crashing force—were succeeded by powerful and dramatic climaxes. Miss Harrison's use of the pedal is sheer wizardry. Time after time the listener was held in rapt admiration by the exceptional effects gained by the pianist through her manipulation of this much-abused part of the pianoforte.

Every performer has his or her own special nightmare of what can go wrong before a concert. One such nightmare materialized for Hazel before that Aeolian Hall performance. She wrote about it to Alain Locke:

May 9

Dear Friend,

Well, the concert is over. Began at 9 o'clock at Aeolian Hall!! The car
gave out in Central Park. Had a puncture and we could not find a vacant
one. I almost died. However, there were three critics there and they remained for the entire program. The *Evening America,* the *Telegram* and
the *Evening Mail.* The balcony was well filled and about eight boxes. Very
enthusiastic audience.

And she continued:

The Aeolian people were lovely and introduced me to a Mr. Isaacson who
has engaged me to play this Friday, May 12 for the *Evening Mail* concert. I
think he said Town Hall. I played for him about an hour ago, and he said I
could also play again May 22 and 23rd. He was very enthusiastic. I am
going to practice all day tomorrow and Thursday at the Steinway
wareroom to get ready. This is my real chance before a fine white audience.
I will not receive money but it means getting before the New York public
and I play two groups. Please hold the thought I will do well.[29]

Sometimes the *Defender* reprinted programs she gave in other
cities:

May 6, 1922

. . . Hazel Harrison, pianist, appeared in recital in St. Louis, Mo.,
at Poro College Auditorium, presented by Gamma Omega chapter
of the Alpha Kappa Alpha sorority. Miss Harrison presented the
following program "Charles" [*sic*] Bach-Busoni; "Maiden's Wish,"
Nocturne ("My Joy"), Chopin-Liszt; "Scherzo," Chopin;
"Fantasia Quasi Sonate," Liszt; "The Chasse," Paganini-Liszt;
"By the Sea," Smetana; "Arabesque," Leschetizsky; "Confessional
Song," Beethoven-Liszt; "Valse de Concert," Donizetti-Liszt.
Miss Harrison, as usual, was a delight to her audience in each
number. The recital was for the purpose of raising money for the
establishment of a scholarship fund for the girls of Sumner High
School. Miss Harrison will be one of the special teachers for the
summer term at the Chicago University of Music.

In July of the same year, Pauline James Lee opened the new quarters of her Chicago University of Music, and this confirmed in many minds that Chicago was indeed the leader in things musical. The successful launching of this mammoth project was the extension of many of Azalia Hackley's ideas and plans, which she never saw realized. There was a total staff of thirty-three, headed by Hazel Harrison and Cornella Lampton (later Mrs. William E. Dawson), piano; Florence Cole Talbert, Antoinette Garnes, and Mary E. Jones, voice; Charles Watts, public-school music; Hazel Thompson Davis, dancing; Carribel Cole Plummer, physical education; George Dewey Lipscomb, dramatic art; Ethel Minor Gavin, history of music. Hazel's own dream had been to open a school of music with her friend Edward Boatner, singer and choral director, but the pressure of both their schedules prevented it, and Boatner eventually gave up his post as choir director at a Chicago church to go to Wiley College in Texas.[30]

On occasion the *Defender* carried sections from reviews of out-of-town concerts:

January 5, 1924

Miss Hazel Harrison has just returned from a successful concert tour, which included Fisk University, Hopkinsville, Ky., Wilberforce University, and Columbus, Ohio.

The *Ohio State Journal* says: "Miss Harrison lived up to advance notices in every particular. She is unusually talented. Her technical equipment is that of the mature artist, while her interpretative gifts are marked by genuine imagination and innate sentiment."

The *Columbus Citizen* says: "Miss Harrison produced a carefully calculated exposition of the Bach-Busoni Toccata in C major, followed by an even better reading of the Chopin C sharp minor Scherzo. Three Liszt transcriptions followed. The third, a Paganini etude, stirred the audience noticeably.

Two unpublished compositions by Elnora Manson, a friend of the pianist, were played from the manuscript. One of these, "A Cabin Cradle Song," was wrought of purely racial traits of the Negro musical nature. "Elftanz" was admirably executed and feelingly interpreted. The fleeting charms of this number were tossed off nimbly, and in the song section she produced a much warmer tone than anything else on the program."

Illinois State Journal: "Hazel Harrison, Colored pianist, played
to an appreciative audience last evening, when she appeared in
recital in the auditorium of the Springfield High School. She
presented a very difficult and interesting program with clarity, spirit,
power, and musical feeling."

The *Defender* was still pressing the matter of employing black
artists to make recordings, and in its regular column "News of the
Music World," written by Hazel's close friend Maude Roberts
George, who had succeeded Nora Douglas Holt, it continued to ask
its patrons to

ask for numbers by Marian Anderson, contralto, and Roland Hayes, tenor.
Both have made records recently, and music lovers should show their
appreciation for high class music rendered by our own artists. The National
Association of Negro Musicians has for several years been trying to
convince the Victor company that numbers other than Blues would have a
large sale.[31]

February 23, 1924

Miss Hazel Harrison, pianist, has returned during the week from a
successful tour in the South and Southwest and will leave the last
of the week for a mid-western tour.

Hazel's own concerns centered around getting engagements,
working out schedules, practicing, pleasing her audiences, and
returning to Europe. She spoke of these frequently in her letters to
Locke, always addressing him as "Dear Friend":

September 16 [no year]

Dear Friend,
    Your letters were forwarded to me in Idlewild, where we spent a
delightful six weeks. I did not touch the piano the entire time, and now am
practicing all day, working on an entirely new program for Fisk. Mr. Tibbs
came over and wanted me to play in Washington under the direction of the
Lincoln Theater. They are having these concerts, six in number, at 5:30 in
the afternoon. Are engaging Hayes, Abbie Mitchell . . . and Jeter. Steinway Grand and pay $150. Everything is supposed to be very fine as to the

piano and audience. How is the standing of the Lincoln Theater?

I hope to hold this engagement off until January. I have a chance to give a concert in Charleston, S.C. then and by that time you will have returned and can tell me what you think of my playing. Walter has gone into another business and is representing the firm in New York. It may be that he will have that territory and then we would live East. In that case, Europe would not be such an effort.

> *Sincerely yours,*
> *Hazel*[32]

January 26 [no year]

Dear Friend,

First of all let me thank you for the beautiful music you sent me from Italy. I play at Biddle tomorrow night, then at Wilmington, N.C., the 22nd, Wilson the 24th, and Petersburg Institute the 26th, Richmond the 28th and then go on to Talladega on Feb. 1. I would come to Washington from Petersburg or after the Richmond concert on the 28th or the 29th. . . . Write in care of President Gandy.

> *Hazel*[33]

June 19 [1922]

Dear Friend,

Your letter to New York was forwarded to me here. I did not stay over the 22nd and 23rd because I played for an Evening Mail concert. . . . I lost my ring also and had spent a lot of time and money on that, so I came directly home. Mr. Diton came over to see me about the Philadelphia concert. . . . I have my new piano, it has a wonderful tone, and I have been working hard for a week on my new program. Am going to teach at the new Music School one or two afternoons until the 7th of August. With the new piano, Europe is out of the question for me this year. . . .

> *Very truly yours*
> *Hazel*[34]

A postcard from Philadelphia:

November 5, 1922

Dear Roy,

We gave Hazel one of the finest recitals ever given in Philadelphia. Three write-ups from the big papers!

> *Carl Diton*

Dear Friend,

    I am so glad they were pleased with the concert last night. I hope I can please the Washington Audience.

Sincerely,
Hazel[35]

November 1 [no year]

Dear Friend,

    Thank you so much for that wonderful letter. We have talked Europe ever since Mr. Heinze wanted me to try out your idea about one year ago, but I did not think I played near well enough. This card is just to tell you that we are looking forward to your visit. Please you are always welcome but I do hope you can make it Christmas because I am home then, so afraid I will be away Easter. . . . I think Mr. Hayes is wonderful. Contact has brought him out. I leave early tomorrow for Philadelphia. I am so nervous about playing there for you. I think I shall stop in Baltimore after the concert there and practice for Washington. I am so anxious to please you. I think of the wonderful music you have heard!! I hope you won't forget anything about Germany. I have to go to New York and on to Rochester and perhaps Syracuse, Indianapolis, on the 23rd. . . . Birdie and Walter send love.

Sincerely,
Hazel[36]

The *Defender* printed the entire review of a concert in Fort Wayne:

March 1, 1924

    Hazel Harrison, Chicago's own pianist, was the recipient of a specially splendid tribute in the Fort Wayne *Journal Gazette*, the daily paper of that city, which reads as follows:

    "Booker T. Washington was the first of the colored race to gain prominence and since then many have risen in their professions, but it remains for Miss Hazel Harrison to stand among her people unrivaled as a pianist. Not only does she stand alone among the Colored people, but she also is at the top with piano artists of all races. A natural talent, years of study and the best of teachers and training have helped her until now she stands recognized and deserving of the word 'artist.'

"There is strength to her playing and her nimble fingering and delicacy of touch form a most effective outlet to her natural talent. Last evening at Packard Hall, where she was presented by the Phyllis Wheatley Social Center, she displayed the minute appreciation of the works of the best composers, and throughout her entire progam there was fluency of remarkable interpretation in her work as well as a desire to create the tone pictures the composers strove for when they wrote the various numbers.

"In the 'Sonate Appationate' [sic] especially, Miss Harrison proved herself to be a brilliant technician, full of sense of rhythmic beauty. . . . 'Elf Tanz' by Sapelnikoff, 'Cabin Song' and 'Serenade' by Rossini-Liszt were delightful selections, played with a delicacy of touch and an appreciation of the finer threads of musical beauty.

"After every group of numbers Miss Harrison was enthusiastically recalled again and again to the stage by the audience who understood and appreciated that an artist was in their midst."

Her appearance in Tuskegee later in March of that year before an audience of 1,500 students, teachers, and members of the community was greeted as "a musical evening of rare excellence. The still, hushed moment following her numbers, before the appreciative applause, revealed best the charm and spell of her performance, which is sympathetic, finished, and radiant."[37] The program on that occasion was:

Scherzo C-sharp Minor	Chopin
"Perpetual Motion"	Weber
Sonata "Appassionata"	Beethoven
Scherzo	Brahms
"Spinning Song"	Schubert-Liszt
Serenade	Rossini-Liszt
Etude E-flat	Paganini-Liszt
"Cabin Song" (from manuscript)	Manson
"Elf Tanz"	Sapelnikov
Arabesque on "Beautiful Blue Danube" Waltz	Strauss-Evler

Returning to Atlanta, this time under the auspices of the Fine
Arts Study Club, Hazel played at the First Congregational Church.
The performance attracted so much attention that a return engagement was requested and arranged, to take place upon her return
from Savannah and towns in Alabama. This time it would be
before a white audience at the Phillips and Crew Music Hall, the
first time it was opened to a colored artist.[38] The music critic of the
Atlanta Journal attended the recital and wrote the following review
of the Congregational Church performance:

> On last Wednesday evening a piano recital was given by the Negro
> pianist, Hazel Harrison, in the Colored First Congregational Church. I had
> the pleasure of hearing this player and was so impressed with the quality of
> her performance that I must give it recognition in this column. Hazel
> Harrison is a pupil of no less a master than the great Busoni, who predicted
> a great pianistic future for her. She presented a program, the technical and
> intellectual magnitude of which would have taxed many masters of
> pianism, and she never faltered once in the task she set for herself.
>
> When I say she played her entire program well, with splendid spontaneity
> and impetuosity of feeling, that she maintained an attitude throughout the
> program of an artist devoted to art, I have not said enough. Perhaps it
> would be better to say that she is a pupil worthy of the great Busoni.
>
> The enormous technical demands of her program were met with astound-
> ing clarity, power and facility. Throughout she manifested superior musical
> intelligence in pedalling and imaginative qualities in interpretation. Her
> rhythm was grace and flexibility itself, in the light airiness of the Elf Tanz
> and in the Arabesque Waltz, or clear cut and vigorous as the character of
> the compositions required. Her chord masses were powerful and of sono-
> rous depth and the entire performance was colorful and virile.
>
> Her playing suggests the masculine more than the feminine. In presence
> she was dignified and modest.
>
> In some southern cities, where she has played in Negro churches, she has
> been called to present a progam to white audiences. A reappearance here
> would give a distinct satisfaction to her audience.[39]

After the repeat performance before an audience of musicians,
she was given an ovation, "and her discriminating audience were
literally carried off their feet by the stupendous accomplishment of
this gifted pianist." A program so intellectually and technically
demanding "had not been played here by any great artist" and she
accomplished it "with ease and distinction. This pianist's tone is

virile, her rhythmic technique is stupendous and her imaginative and emotional qualities are highly developed."[40]

Hazel's 1924 tour ended with a recital in Chicago in April, at Grace Presbyterian Church, sponsored by Theta Omega Chapter of Alpha Kappa Alpha Sorority. It was a musical and social occasion, and Maude Roberts George reported that "music lovers and society were out *en masse* to greet Miss Harrison and the wonderful audience must have been a great inspiration to her." She further noted that "the program was one which only a truly great artist would have attempted, and because of their difficulty some of the numbers are seldom heard."[41]

In addition to the selections from her regular repertoire, Hazel had included on the program two compositions by her friend Elnora Manson, "Hermit's Song" and "Cabin Song." They had appeared often on the programs of this year's tour and had received particular mention in the reviews. On this occasion, the composer was in the audience and was given prolonged applause at the conclusion, when her presence became known. Maude Roberts George declared that "too much cannot be said in praise of Miss Harrison's art. She is a born musician and also has the gift of rare interpretative ability." In closing her review, she gives the reader the feeling of being there:

. . . the entire audience was spellbound, so intently did they listen. There was perfect interpretation of Chopin, then Elf Tanz, which requires delicacy and brilliance, the smoothness and coloring of the Serenade proving the musical soul of this artist, rarely interpreted and thoroughly felt by the audience. Perpetual Motion was rendered with such assurance and brilliance, as well as unusual rapidity, as to prove Miss Harrison's virtuoso command of the keyboard. Arabesque on Beautiful Blue Danube, the closing number, which contains tunes that are familiar to music lovers was beautifully rendered and was so enthusiastically applauded by the audience that Miss Harrison was forced to respond with an encore. There was prolonged and enthusiastic applause throughout the program and Miss Harrison has attained the prophecy of Mr. Busoni that she would become a truly great artist. She reflects great credit upon her distinguished teacher.

Her lovely mother, who accompanied her abroad to study, was present at the recital and deserves congratulations for having the foresight to develop the talent of her daughter. Theta Omega chapter is to be congratulated upon their first public attempt toward a scholarship fund and they were particularly fortunate in their selection of an artist.[42]

The year 1925 was equally successful. After recitals in Winnipeg, Canada, and Des Moines in January, she went south for two months. Her performance at Wiley College in Marshall, Texas,

bore strong confirmation of the wide reputation which she sustains both in America and Europe as an artist of the first magnitude. Through the entire program of one hour and a half, consisting of the most highly technical compositions, Miss Harrison maintained a pre-eminence that was readily discernible in the minds even of the lay members of her audience.[43]

"I play in La Porte this coming Thursday and after that am concentrating on Europe. Am practicing always."[44] The return to La Porte in June 1925 was not that of the hometown girl on the threshold of a promising career, but of a successful and mature concert artist whose acclaim around the country had only seconded what La Porteans had known all along. It was the kind of homecoming that every artist hardly dares to dream about, and it must have been one of the most heartwarming times she ever knew. The reviewer for the *La Porte Herald-Argus* (25 June 1925) acknowledged that

the applause which greeted the former La Porte girl was not the ordinary acknowledgement of the casual audience for a great artist nor was it mere appreciation of the attractive picture Miss Harrison completed as she stood before the mulberry curtain in her gown of rose sequins, chiffon, and silver. It was not the ear-splitting noise which arose from more than 500 pairs of hands which so overwhelmed her, for she has long since become accustomed to praise from some of the most exclusive musical circles of Europe and America. No, it was not the noise that almost robbed her of her poise, but the warmth of the reception and the smiles on the faces of the audience before her that touched the heart of the artist.

Her program opened with three Bach-Busoni chorales, and at their conclusion she was recalled

again and again to acknowledge the laudation from the assembly and to receive two beautiful bunches of roses. Miss Harrison murmured as she reached for the buds, "I can't say a word!" As the program progressed, the bunches of roses on the piano became mounds of roses, and she finally had to ask for a chair to put them on.

At the end of the recital, she had hardly left the piano when the crowd pressed in and surrounded her, many of them old acquaintances and high-school friends. All the hometown folks were proud to grasp her hand and call her "Hazel."

The reviewer noted that her work was marked by a "depth and fullness of tone probably unexcelled by any other woman pianist of the present day." His awe at her power and facile technique and transparent clarity simply stated one more time what all reviewers had been impelled to comment on, and for this occasion it was the Chopin F Minor Fantasie and Weber's "Perpetual Motion" that provided the opportunity. Most impressive on this occasion was her playing of the Liszt "St. Francis Walking on the Waves," which she made even more enjoyable for her audience by recounting for them, before she interpreted the story on the piano, the legend of St. Francis and the boatman. Her program concluded with the Schulz-Evler "Concert Arabesques on Theme of By the Beautiful Blue Danube" (Strauss), a composition that, over the years, would become closely identified with her and that audiences would frequently ask for as an encore. On this occasion, however, she played "By the Sea" by Smetana as the encore.

Among the old friends who welcomed Hazel after the recital were Florence Low, now a young matron, and Florence Andrew, who had her own piano studio and pupils. They greeted each other warmly and affectionately and conversed for a while. When they parted, it was as if none of the years had intervened as Hazel said to them, "Now, girls, go home and practice, practice!"[45]

One of the great pleasures that Hazel enjoyed as a deviation from her busy schedule was the annual visit to Idlewild, Michigan, a favorite summer retreat of the time. She and Birdie had purchased a cabin there, and each year they spent from four to six weeks in their "log cabin." There was no piano there, but that was part of the plan; this was a time for rest and relaxation. Birdie often said to Hazel, "Now, Hazel, one month out of the year there just ought to be a time when you do absolutely nothing." They were located on the water and had the use of a boat, and their daily regime consisted of rowing and relaxing; reading; rowing and relaxing. But Hazel's compulsion to musical activity could not stand a month's abstention, and she used to confide to friends that she would "take some music and look at the notes."[46]

She continued to concentrate on Europe. Writing Locke to thank him for sending her the issue of *Survey Graphic* that contained his widely discussed article, "Enter the New Negro," she ruminated:

I have just about decided to Europe. . . . Mr. Busoni being dead, I am a little undecided whether to go to London first, or go to Holland to Petri. Perhaps Mr. Hayes knows someone who might be interested. I want to go over as soon after August 1st as I can. Am practicing always. Had a fine concert in Cleveland and also in St. Louis in May. Am trying to keep two old programs up to concert pitch and learn a new one.

Birdie and Walter are well. The latter is going into the cosmetic business. About the third venture in the last three years. . . . While South this winter I had a touch of malaria or flu anyhow I lost nineteen pounds. Birdie thinks I look a lot more like I used to.

Please write because I am so anxious about Europe. Is it cheaper to leave from Canada, New York or Philadelphia?[47]

In another letter to Locke:

Mr. Heinze my old German teacher is in Cleveland for six weeks. He wrote me he hoped to play here. Has had time for practice in Europe. My chance is in Europe. Have worked out some new principals [sic] which have helped my work.[48]

By November, her plans were almost complete:

Things seem to be opening up for me, and I hope to get off for Europe in January. I have written to Mr. Petri in Holland but do not know whether he is there or in Berlin. If I do not hear from him, will go on with Mr. Heinze's idea. He wants me to polish up one or two programs and concertize. He is in Munich and very anxious that I come at once, but I cannot go before the first of the year.[49]

There were details to attend to: selling the piano, storing some things at Idlewild. This time, Birdie would remain at home. On the last day of 1925 she sailed for Germany.

* * *

The *Westphalia* left early, and Hazel, accompanied by a Mrs. Mitchell, was excited as she waved to her friends, Dr. Locke and

Mr. Mitchell, who had come to see them off. "Each minute I am happier," she confided. "If it wasn't for Birdie, I would never think of America again."[50] She wrote enthusiastically of life aboard the ship:

There are twenty-four genial Germans in our cabin. We are a great curiosity to them. We did not remain for the dance last night, but I will go in for the moving pictures this evening. . . . I am walking twelve times around our part of the boat after each meal, and trying to control my appetite. (Very difficult the last). I have studied two hours daily on some of the new compositions.[51]

A few days later, another letter from shipboard added:

The concertmeister's wife of Mengleberg's orchestra of New York is on board. We are quite good friends and she plays quite well—has given me much information. The captain gave the most elaborate dinner last night! It was followed by a dance. We land tomorrow morning. Remain a day or so in Hamburg for a concert then on to southern Germany. . . . I have talked a great deal of German. Find myself talking German to Mrs. Mitchell. She is *so* charming. A delightful companion. . . . I am still happier each day. . . . How you would have enjoyed these people![52]

Hazel made a number of friends on this trip. One fellow shared with her his interest in folksongs and in the Negro; another, a mining engineer who had been in China for eighteen years, told her of China and its customs. Another passenger, in the process of reorganizing a publishing house in New York, was interested in conditions among Negroes in the United States and sought information of books on this subject. There was also a composer who offered to get a Grotrian Steinway for her use, as

Petri and all of the big artists use this piano. . . . After I am up to concert pitch I am to play for them and he is sure things can be arranged so that the piano question is settled. I think he wants me to play some of his compositions which I am very glad to do.[53]

Berlin, 1926. Eleven years had passed since Hazel had last seen Berlin. A world of memories crowded in on her as she visited the old familiar places she had so often frequented when Berlin was the musical center of the world. Outwardly, there was little change in the city; there was more street traffic, but the principal streets—Unter der Linden, Friedrichstrasse, Leipzigstrasse, Potsdamerstrasse—looked as they did before the war. Business, however, was in a serious depression, and the life and bustle so characteristic of Berlin before the war had ceased to be: the trains were now half empty, there were few customers in department stores and restaurants, and there was a great falling off in concert attendance.[54] Hazel wrote back to her friend Maude Roberts George that "the communist people [are] greatly in evidence."[55] New York had replaced Berlin as the musical center of the world, not only in musical activity, but in famous resident musicians as well. Busoni had died, as had Nikisch, Max Bruch, Humperdinck, and others; but new names were appearing on the scene. The Philharmonic was retaining its old supremacy, and the venerable Singakademie, the scene of Hazel's debut, was still in use as a concert hall.

Some of the changes were less evident in Munich, whose "beauty as an art center is unsurpassed. There one enjoys the ideal German life."[56] Concert patrons were wooed with a decrease in ticket prices and an increase in the production of operas. Alban Berg's *Wozzeck* was finally viewed after 137 rehearsals,[57] and Hindemith's *Cardillac* was produced;[58] elsewhere, Busoni's posthumous opera, *Faust*, had a fine reception.[59] The centenary of Carl Maria von Weber's death was commemorated by a festival at his home town of Eutin (Mecklenburg);[60] in Monte Carlo, Honegger's *Judith* received its premiere.[61] Another development of interest was the use of films as music-teaching aids. These films, developed by the Berlin State Conservatory, were so successful that they were made available to the general public at special performances.[62]

Hazel renewed her ties with Egon Petri, whose fame as a soloist and a teacher was now well established. In addition to carrying on the Busoni tradition in pianoforte playing, he had performed with Busoni and collaborated with him on an edition of Bach's clavier works. In 1923 he had been the first foreign artist to play in Soviet Russia, where his success was such that he had to perform thirty-one times during forty days.[63] After many successful tours, he had finally settled in Berlin as a teacher at the Berlin Hochschule für Musik, with some advanced private pupils of his own. He was especially pleased to work with Hazel again.

In late October 1926, after ten months, Hazel sailed from Hamburg for New York on the *Cleveland*, and arrived there on November 8. She found the billboards filled with program publicity for Myra Hess's "only New York concert," Galli-Curci, Lawrence Tibbett, Rosa Ponselle, Alfred Cortot, Percy Grainger playing the Duo-Art Reproducing Piano, bandmaster Edwin Goldman, and Tito Schipa. The names of major management agencies, such as Hurok, Judson, Culbertson, Aeolian Company, Friedberg, Daniel Mayer, Inc., and the Metropolitan Musical Bureau were well known. Many artists clamored for their attention and backing, for in this highly competitive climate, effective management meant the difference between success and failure.

About this same time, two Native Americans were enjoying a large amount of publicity. Tsiaina, a Cherokee, and Oskenonton, a Mohawk, were featured in concerts from coast to coast. It was Charles Wakefield Cadman who brought further recognition to Tsiaina by writing an opera based on her life and in which she sang the title role.[64] The team of J. Rosamond Johnson and Taylor Gordon also enjoyed favorable notices. Appearing in concerts featuring Negro spirituals, Johnson and Gordon's performances were enthusiastically received. Feature articles called attention to their work in this area and to the forthcoming publication of their second book of American Negro spirituals.[65]

At this homecoming, Hazel again found herself very much in demand, and she enjoyed full bookings over the next several years. She brought to her audiences a repertoire recognized for its brilliance and technical difficulty. She brought them the grand literature of Germany, Russia, and Poland, and many works that were not yet included in the standard concert repertory. These included unpublished works of composers considered avant garde in their day, as well as works by black composers of her acquaintance—Elnora Manson, William Dawson, Dean Dixon, and Hall Johnson. She introduced her audiences to the "color music" of Alexander László, which she had heard him play in Germany on the piano of his own invention, which threw upon a screen the colors corresponding to the music in their proportional wave lengths. Although Hazel did not include the projection of colors onto a screen as she played the music, the László "Color Impressions" was always an audience-pleaser, and she retained it in her repertoire for years. The keyboard representations of blue, green, violet, gray, and red must have been stunning. Mrs. John Work of Nashville recalled, in 1980, how she had heard Hazel Harrison play the color music in the late 1920s in Charleston, South Carolina, and how vivid the memory of it has remained with her through the years. Hazel did, however, confide once to Florence Andrew that she found the "white" section the most difficult to play with conviction, as it was so bland. Hazel herself, so gay and lively, had much more affinity for the red.

In April 1929, a very special honor came to Hazel. She was among a number of women recognized at a ceremony in the chapel of the University of Chicago. Sponsored by the YWCA as part of a leadership-of-women conference program, the ceremony paid tribute to women of all races in business, social work, public affairs, education, religion, the arts, literature, medicine, the law, and government. It was a brilliant ceremony: the women marching down the aisle, the organ pealing out the processional on a theme by Handel, the pews filled with an admiring audience. Among the honorees were Elizabeth Lindsay Davis, pioneer organizer and historian, her hand in that of Amelia Sears, internationally known social worker and head of the United Charities; Ida B. Wells Barnett, the "mother of clubs," wearing her black gown with all dignity; Mary McLeod Bethune of Bethune-Cookman College was a special guest; and Hazel Harrison "held her place in the realm of music with her sisters of whiter skin."[66]

We have invited as guests," said Rev. Dean Charles Whitney Gilkey,

those who share the spirit of the idealism of this university. In this service, expressive of the leadership of women, the university shares heartily in this welcome more gladly and more appropriately since the university owes so much to the rich influences which have been brought through the lives of many of its women.

Margaret E. Burton of the YWCA's national board defined the service as representative of the women of the present and, through them, the womanhood of the future "who can be claimed by no one nation, but belong to the world."[67] The epoch-making ceremony of song and litany was solemn and impressive, and Hazel regarded it for the rest of her life as the finest honor she ever received.

A big year for Hazel was 1930. One of the major musical events of the 1929-1930 New York season was her appearance there on Sunday afternoon January 19 at International House. It was the first stop on her winter tour, and her appearance there was under the management of Mrs. Carl Diton, well-known concert promoter and wife of the gifted Negro pianist. Cleveland Allen, who covered the New York music scene for the *Chicago Defender*, declared the recital to be one of the most notable artistic triumphs that he had ever witnessed. "It was," he said, "one of the most outstanding events in New York that season, and drew a distinguished audience of music patrons, including Dr. Robert R. Moton of Tuskegee, who gave her a genuine ovation that told of the place she has in the hearts of the music lovers of the country."

"Her playing," Allen continued,

was noted for its remarkable technique and tonal coloring, with exquisite shading and a rare style of interpretation. Her playing is most individual and she shows the result of superior training and brings to her art the finest artistry and expression. She offered a well-balanced program, which had been carefully selected and which gave her every opportunity to appear to the highest advantage. She gave one of the highest demonstrations of pianoforte playing that has ever been heard here, and justified her reputation of being one of the foremost pianists of the country.[68]

With another successful concert season behind her, Hazel was awarded, in the summer of 1930, a special Chicago Musical College scholarship for study with Percy Grainger, the internationally famous concert pianist and teacher. He later made a statement about her that she used frequently in her promotional literature: "There is room for her in the music world, for she will be at the top."

A New York recital opened her 1930 fall tour. This one was special as it was her Town Hall debut. A Town Hall recital had become obligatory for any serious artist, and so it was with Hazel, although she was now forty-seven and well past the debut stage of her life. The major portion of the program consisted of Siloti's arrangement of Bach's Prelude in E Minor, Liszt's Variations on a

Bach Theme, Chopin's B Minor Sonata, Brahms' Intermezzi in C
Major and B-flat Minor and the E-flat Rhapsodie.

The concert was covered by the major New York papers. The
Telegram (16 October 1930) reported that "beginning with Siloti's
arrangement of Bach's Prelude in E minor, Miss Harrison straight-
away disclosed a sound musicianship and training. . . . She played
with a delicate feeling for nuance and color . . . a technical display
of amazing breadth and intricacy." The *New York American* (16
October 1930) noted that "she is a musician with taste and talent.
. . . Her interpretation of Chopin's B Minor Sonata contained
much that was commendable in tone quality, phrasing and
expression." The *Herald Tribune* (16 October 1930) merely stated
that her technique was accurate and her tone agreeable. The *Sun*
(16 October 1930): "Miss Harrison . . . disclosed a good piano
tone, musical temperament and seriousness." The reviewer for the
Times 16 (October 1930) singled out her "full and singing tone and
deft pedalling" for comment, mentioning a few details that he felt
detracted, such as the "clipping of sixteenth and thirty-second
notes between rapid ornamental passages." Overall, "the impression of a serious musician remained."

Hazel remained in New York for a few days, relaxing, visiting,
and being entertained by her many friends. The next big
engagement to fulfill was at Boston's Jordan Hall on November 25.
It was still unusual for a Negro artist to make such an appearance
there. Passing out flyers advertising Hazel's forthcoming recital
was John Orth, who many years before had been a pupil of Liszt,
and whose studio was in Steinert Hall on Boylston Street. It was in
this same building that the Steinway people had their showroom,
with studios upstairs occupied by various private teachers. Orth, a
man of very strong social conscience, maintained a studio there, as
did Nicolas Slonimsky, whom Koussevitzky had brought to Boston
to serve as official pianist and researcher to the Boston Symphony
Orchestra.[69]

Hazel met Orth and Slonimsky in Boston. Writing from the
Woman's Community Club, where she was stopping, she mentions
having played for John Orth.

He has been wonderful, arranged at once for me to play for Mr. Chadwick
who said he would help me in any way he could, kept me playing for him

for an hour and a half. . . . I also met Slonimsky who was very favorably impressed and wants me to play some of his compositions as yet unpublished. A marked rhythm, very difficult. He is having three Spanish things copied, so I can get them Monday next. Also met Leginska's manager and played for him. . . . I am to practice in the retiring room of the conductor. So quiet and a wonderful Steinway.[70]

Such were the events leading to the concert in Boston. She appeared before a "fair-sized, very enthusiastic audience," and the reviews were mixed, with lukewarm being the most positive. The *Boston Post* (26 November 1930) felt that "her playing too often lacked law and order; there was vagueness of rhythm, and Miss Harrison seemed to lose her way in the music." The *Globe* (26 November 1930) referred to her well-known, "if not always clean cut technique" and wished for "more profundity, more attention to technical details, more regard for the spiritual and emotional content of her music than she now displays." The condescending review of the *Evening Transcript* (26 November 1930) noted:

Since her recital of last season, Miss Hazel Harrison, pianist, has made some progress as an interpretative musician and has maintained the considerable technical ability which she then displayed. Last evening in Jordan Hall, improvements were noted, particularly in Chopin's Sonata in B Minor. She played the Allegro in good rhythm, clearly brought out the melody and intelligently distributed the harmony. In the Scherzo, she dashed off the closing measures with well-taught assurance, and for the closing movement was able to summon sufficient impetuosity. She likewise seemed to appreciate the significance of the whole design. Then, there were flashes of lucid playing in the Intermezzo in B-flat Minor of Brahms, while the Rhapsody in E-flat Major by the same composer lacked nothing in emphatic pace.

On the whole, however, Miss Harrison has yet to develop a more rational performance. In the first number of her program, Siloti's arrangement of a Prelude from Bach, she disclosed the weighty attack which was to prevail throughout the evening. The first movement from Chopin's Sonata . . . was inclined to be ponderous and muddy. The Largo was thickly pedalled. In fact, all of the slower and more solemn divisions of the Sonata proceeded rather cumbersomely. And to complete the list of shortcomings—in the Intermezzo in C Major of Brahms, she entirely missed the ·natural lilt which is the most engaging characteristic of the piece, preferring, instead, an erratic and oddly placed accent.

There remains for commendation, Miss Harrison's technical equipment. She seems to be able to encompass any given amount of music at top speed and with overwhelming power. In swift passage work, her fingers are agile and accurate; for music of depth and sonority, she possesses sufficient muscularity. She enjoys grappling heartily with her music, thus displaying a quality which, if properly directed, will increase her abilities.

Unfortunately, these reviewers did not discuss the rest of her program, for it revealed another facet of Hazel's repertoire. On this particular concert, the final portion of the program was devoted entirely to music of contemporaries, some of whom she had only recently met:

"Elf Tanz"	Sapelnikov
"Dreamy Dells" (after Tennyson)	John Orth
"Imperia Silhouettes Iberiennes" (from manuscript)	Slonimsky
"One More Day, My John" (sea chanty)	Grainger
Paraphrase (Tschaikowsky's "Flower Waltz")	Grainger

Hazel was indisputably an early advocate of twentieth-century music, a champion of the lesser-known composer. She carried out her promises to composers to premiere new works, and she regularly programmed these compositions. "In the last several years," commented Josephine Harreld Love, "I have been able to appreciate to such an extent how advanced Hazel was. Composers who are now considered very much a part of the music spectrum, at that time were not—Prokofieff, Scriabin, Schönberg. . . . My early exposure to those composers was through her."[71]

Hazel completed another full concert season in the spring of 1931. She won a scholarship with Mme. Sina Lichtmann, a Russian, of New York. This seemed to have been a propitious time for her to change her base of operations. New York offered expanded opportunities and a more intense musical life than Chicago did. Then, too, the marriage to Walter Anderson had ended two years before, he divorcing her. So Hazel made the decision to move to New York, and Birdie would go with her.

But it was not to be. William Dawson had been given carte blanche by Robert R. Moton, president of Tuskegee Institute, to put together a music school that would be second to none. Already a friend of Hazel's through his late wife, as well as a fellow Chicago musician, Dawson made an offer to Hazel to head the school's Piano Department. Hazel accepted. Perhaps after fifteen years of concertizing she wanted to try teaching again; perhaps audiences were changing. The economic security of teaching during a deepening recession was almost certainly a factor. So instead of heading east to New York, she turned south to Alabama.

1. The young Hazel at the time of her debut with the Berlin Philharmonic Orchestra, 1904. *From the Collections of the Library of Congress.*

2. Hazel Harrison, "premiere pianiste." *Schomburg Center for Research in Black Culture, New York Public Library, Astor, Lenox and Tilden Foundations.*

3. The internationally acclaimed pianist, a pupil of Busoni and Petri. *Schomburg Center for Research in Black Culture, New York Public Library, Astor, Lenox and Tilden Foundations.*

4. With colleagues of the School of Music at Howard University in the early 1950s. *Courtesy of the Moorland-Spingarn Research Center, Howard University.*

5. The Tuskegee School of Music faculty, 1934–1935. *Courtesy of Willliam L. Dawson.*

6. "Symphony Under the Stars." Hazel is pictured here with Ellabelle Davis and Lena Horne, conductor Izler Solomon, officials of the National Association of Negro Musicians, and members of the Hollywood Bowl Orchestra; 1949. *Courtesy of the Moorland-Spingarn Research Center, Howard University.*

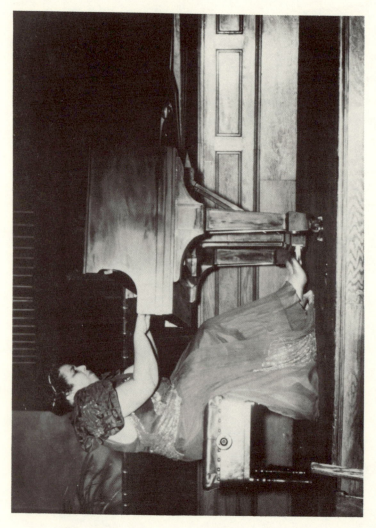

7. "The dean of native pianists." *Courtesy of Mary O. H. Williamson, Moorland-Spingarn Research Center, Howard University.*

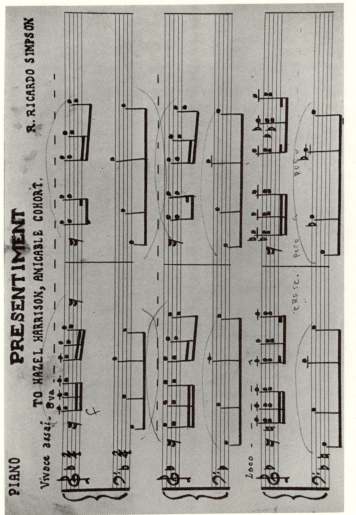

8. "Presentiment," written for Hazel and dedicated to her by Ralph Simpson. *Courtesy of Ralph Simpson.*

9. Hazel in 1957 at the age of seventy-four. *Reprinted by permission of the Johnson Publishing Company, Inc.*

10. Bowing at her last performance in 1959. *Courtesy of the Moorland-Spingarn Research Center, Howard University.*

4

TUSKEGEE INSTITUTE: 1931-1936

Tuskegee Institute and Hazel were no strangers to each other; she had made concert appearances on its spacious and attractive campus, and Tuskegee was pleased to have this famous artist join its faculty. The new School of Music was part of Tuskegee's curriculum expansion, which included upgraded vocational education and an enlarged liberal arts program, emphasizing what the school did well: music. Already established on campus were a well-known concert band, a choir of one hundred voices, an orchestra with full instrumentation, a girls' glee club of fifty voices, a men's glee club of seventy voices, and the Tuskegee Quartet, which went on regular tours around the country.[1]

The School of Music was established in 1931, and when Principal Moton and William Dawson finally agreed on terms, Dawson returned to Tuskegee as the school's director. So important was the new school to the institution that, at one of the Sunday evening chapel services, the assistant to the principal, G. Lake Imes, announced its formation to the assembled students and faculty. Then, in order to underscore its importance, he further announced that the director's salary would be second only to the president's.[2] Afterward, there was a good deal of grumbling among the faculty, but it subsided shortly since those were the days when good teaching jobs were scarce and grumbling too loudly or too long was hazardous to job security.

For his faculty, Dawson recruited some of the most illustrious musicians of the day. Among them were Abbie Mitchell, who had enjoyed successful concert and musical-comedy careers here and abroad, who came as head of voice culture and repertoire; Andrew Rosemond, violinist, who was appointed director of the orchestra; and, of course, Hazel. The well-known Captain Drye was already on hand as band leader of the widely acclaimed and widely traveled Tuskegee band. Other able musicians on the faculty were Orrin Suthern, organist, and Catherine Moton Patterson, Oberlin Conservatory graduate and daughter of the president. Portia Washington Pittman, Booker T's daughter, had returned to Tuskegee in 1928 after her marriage to Sidney Pittman had broken up, and she taught piano and directed the choir until Dawson took over its direction. Joining the faculty later would be Florence Cole Talbert, well known at home and abroad for her operatic and oratorio appearances and as an energetic recitalist as well.

It was a homecoming of sorts for Abbie Mitchell and Portia Pittman. They had become friends years before, when Portia was living in Berlin and Abbie stopped there for a while on her concert tour of the major European capitals. It was natural that the two of them, with so much in common—young, musically talented, away from home—should become fast friends. Their friendship was renewed when they found themselves at Tuskegee in the same department. Many pleasant times were spent in each other's company, Portia playing the piano and helping Abbie with her German as she sang lieder and selections from the German operas.[3] Although Portia and Hazel had not lived in Berlin at the same time, they had both lived at 58 Steglitzerstrasse with the same landlady, and they had a mutual love for the German people and language. They were both pianists with an innate pianistic sense. While Portia later recalled that, at Tuskegee, "we knew each other intimately and we talked our secrets together," there may have been a touch of self-bolstering in the light of Hazel and Abbie's successful public careers when she remarked, "I had the advantage because I had more education. They had music, but they had never gone very far in school, Hazel especially."[4] Portia and Hazel, both anxious to retain their fluency in German, must have turned more than a few heads as they strolled across the Tuskegee campus speaking German.[5]

Fitting these individual artists, some of whom had never had academic exposure before, into an academic framework was not easy for Dawson. Eventually, however, courses were developed, performance standards set and made known, and a solid four-year curriculum leading to a bachelor of music degree was in place. In the Piano Department, there was, in addition, a division for children under thirteen years and a preparatory division for students over thirteen, including beginners.

After a concert at the Morningside Residence Club in New York in the fall of 1931, Hazel moved to Tuskegee; Birdie remained in Chicago. Hazel already knew many of the Tuskegee residents and, having grown up in La Porte, was amenable to small-town life. She settled into a faculty dormitory and was provided a studio with a new Steinway on the lower floor of the Collis B. Huntington Memorial Building.

Thus began this new phase of her career. Her pupils were, for the most part, those who were enrolled through the School of Music—the children, the preparatory, and the conservatory students—but there were also advanced students who came regularly from Montgomery and Atlanta. Two of her Montgomery pupils were Portia Trenholm, wife of the president of Alabama State College, and Mary Hatcher Goldsmith, a Howard alumna who taught music at the college, both of whom would become her colleagues years later.

Another student, on whom she had an extraordinarily strong and lasting influence, was a young trumpeter majoring in music, who later wrote in the *American Scholar* of the insight she transmitted to him almost in the form of a riddle. In a conversation that he never forgot, Hazel advised a crestfallen Ralph Ellison to *"always* play your best, even if it's only in the waiting room at Chehaw Station, because in this country there will always be a little man hidden behind the stove . . . and he'll know the *music*, and the *tradition*, and the standards of musicianship of *whatever* it is you set out to perform"; that no matter how isolated or unlikely the circumstances, there is almost always an "unaccountable knowingness" on the part of someone—not to forget it, baby, and "always prepare yourself to play your very best wherever you are, and on all occasions."[6]

Tuskegee was a cultural and economic oasis in rural Alabama, of necessity self-contained and self-sufficient. While more or less isolated geographically, it was situated between Montgomery and

Atlanta and was reasonably well served by bus and by the Atlanta and West Point Railroad. Travelers disembarked at woebegone Chehaw, where the Tuskegee train took them the remaining five miles to Tuskegee Institute. In Booker T. Washington's day, many prominent figures from the larger educational and political world visited Tuskegee at his invitation. Later, touring artists found it a welcome stop on their itineraries, often remaining a day or so beyond their engagement date in order to relax with the Motons, meet Dr. Carver, or hear the choir in rehearsal or in performance at Sunday chapel.

With the completion of Logan Hall in 1931, there was now on campus a modern and spacious facility to accommodate the large crowds that came to the campus for Founder's Day, Commencement Day, the Farmers' Conference, the clinics, and athletic exhibitions of various kinds. The Entertainment Course, which, since 1920, had brought many distinguished artists to the campus, could now offer greatly improved facilities. Over the years, this series had brought to the campus such attractions as the Russian Symphony Orchestra, the St. Louis Symphony Orchestra, Martha Graham and her Dance Ensemble, John Philip Sousa and his band, the Abby Theatre Irish Players, Andrés Segovia, Roland Hayes, Marian Anderson, Mme. Schumann-Heink, the entire cast of *Green Pastures*, and band leaders Duke Ellington, Noble Sissle, and W. C. Handy.

The Minneapolis Symphony Orchestra had appeared at Tuskegee in 1931, performing to a capacity audience in the chapel. Its appearance the following year, under the baton of Eugene Ormandy, marked the formal opening of Logan Hall. Busloads and carloads came from Talladega College, Alabama State College, Auburn Polytechnic Institute, Tuskegee High School, Fort Benning, Columbus, Opelika, Union Springs, Birmingham, and Selma.[7] Kemper Harreld brought five carloads from Atlanta.[8] In all, 2,200 people were on hand to hear the Minneapolis Symphony Orchestra concert, which opened with the overture to *Tannhäuser* and the Schubert "Unfinished" Symphony. Of primary interest was the orchestra's presentation of Nathaniel Dett's "Juba" and Hazel's appearance as soloist with the orchestra. In this way, Ormandy honored a black composer and a black pianist—a rare occurrence in those days. Hazel played the first movement of the Grieg A

Minor Concerto, without rehearsal, to the great satisfaction and surprise of Mr. Ormandy and the orchestra. In his review of the performance in the *Tuskegee Messenger* (January 1932), William Dawson said that she "proved to be a pianist superb. Seldom has a Tuskegee audience heard such fine, clear, clean, wholesome playing. Her technique is flawless; she combines brain and skill in a most uncommon way."

Hazel appeared on numerous programs at Tuskegee. There were many occasions and visiting dignitaries for which the talents of the music-school faculty and students were displayed. However, her day-to-day responsibility was for her students, as she led them through the requirements of their course of study. A sophomore, for example, would be expected to perform all scales with rapidity and variety of tone (seven notes to a beat, MM96), seventh-chord arpeggios (four notes to a beat, MM132); to have finished at least twelve studies from Czerny opus 740; to be able to perform one of the preludes and fugues from the Bach *Well-Tempered Clavier*, one movement of a sonata equivalent in difficulty to the Beethoven opus 10 no. 3, and a composition from the Romantic period of similar difficulty.[9]

For her personal time, she carved out a schedule similar to the one she had maintained in La Porte years before: sleeping in the early evening and arising to practice at 2 or 3 A.M. She would leave the dormitory and cross the campus to her studio, open it, and practice undisturbed until her first student arrived, about 7:30 A.M. Her compulsion to practice and keep herself up to concert pitch was even more of a necessity now. Although part of her arrangement with Dawson was that she would be free to go on tours,[10] which she continued to do regularly and successfully—she was still the "premiere pianiste"—the additional responsibility of teaching made it necessary for her to return to her old ways of squeezing as many hours for practicing as possible from twenty-four. It meant pinching off sleeping time and having no social life at all, but she had never chosen to have that anyway. A later colleague of Hazel's, Mildred Hall, spoke of Hazel's sleep-teach-practice routine:

> She was a practice maniac. She wore you *out* practicing. They had a joke on her, how she went down to select a piano for one of her recitals somewhere. When the piano was loaded and the driver got in the truck, she

was already at the piano practicing. When you went to your lessons, it was seldom that you got a chance to talk to her afterwards. She was either practicing or resting, mostly practicing, and she expected you to do that, too. The majority of her students were studying [other subjects] too, and they just didn't have that type of devotion that she did. One had other things to do. Practice! Practice! PRACTICE![11]

Yet there were times when she did relax. From time to time, the tightness of the Tuskegee community closed in on Hazel, and having to live the exemplary life became oppressive. She would confide to a friend, "Baby, I'm tired of being a living example. I've got to shake loose and go to New Orleans,"[12] where she would be out from under campus pressures and could relax with friends. More than likely, all she did was to practice. Summers she would return to Chicago and then to Idlewild, enjoying the freedom with Birdie and the Kemper Harreld family.

One of the highlights of the period that Hazel and Abbie Mitchell were at Tuskegee was a joint recital, sponsored by the Entertainment Course and held in Logan Hall. As might be expected, relationships among the music faculty were not without friction. While Abbie and Hazel were friends, they were, nevertheless, friendly rivals as well as artists who could be temperamental. Each one had a following, and on the evening of the recital, a large and enthusiastic group of students, faculty, and visitors was present in Logan Hall. Hazel had top billing for this concert, and appeared first on the program, alternating with Abbie throughout the evening. It was a long and demanding program for Hazel, and had included the Liszt "Dante" Sonata, the intricate "Color Impressions" of László, and several Chopin compositions, among other offerings. But there was fierce competition as to who would be on stage last. Abbie appeared last on the program in a set of four songs, but Hazel felt that she must be the last one to appear on stage. Abbie felt the same way. Each had prearranged with friends in the audience to send notes backstage requesting encores. Abbie's friends wanted to hear her sing "Only a Rose," and Hazel's friends felt that she *must* play the "Blue Danube."[13] It appears that Hazel had the last appearance, as the account in the *Messenger* mentions the "Blue Danube," but not Abbie's "Only a Rose."

Hazel remained at Tuskegee until 1936, when an offer came from

Howard University in Washington, D.C. Hazel was now fifty-three. Since the future of the School of Music was under a cloud, and Washington was closer to the center of the musical world, Hazel decided to accept the offer. Besides, Washington would be more acceptable to Birdie, and she could join Hazel there.

When it was finally time to go and she was about to leave the studio for the last time, Dawson came over to say goodbye. When he glanced at the piano that had been assigned to Hazel when it was new, he could not believe his eyes: the ivory on the keys had been worn down to the wood![14]

5

HOWARD UNIVERSITY: 1936–1955

Miss Hazel L. Harrison was employed in the School of Music from September 1936 until September 1955. Miss Harrison retired June 30, 1954, but was reappointed and worked in the Piano Department until September 1, 1955. Also, she was granted sabbatical leave from September 1, 1947, to June 30, 1950. She was promoted through the ranks of Instructor, Assistant Professor to Associate Professor, with annual salaries ranging from $1,800.00 to $5,250.00. Indefinite tenure was granted to Miss Harrison on September 1, 1947.

> —From the minutes of the Executive Committee of the Board of Trustees, Howard University.[1]

Hazel found a natural home at Howard University. With its thirteen schools and colleges, it was frequently called "the capstone of higher education for Negroes." On its faculty were some of the country's most eminent black scholars: Kelly Miller, Ernest Everett Just, Howard Thurman, Charles Wesley, Sterling Brown, Ralph Bunche, Benjamin Mays, Charles Drew, Benjamin Brawley, and many others, as well as her old friend Alain Locke. News of her coming created a certain air of excitement on campus. Lillian Allen was ecstatic; at last, she would meet the famous Hazel Harrison. "I had read a great deal about her and was on edge to hear her. I had heard Rachmaninoff and Paderewski, and now I would hear another great pianist—a woman, a black woman."[2]

Hazel was pleased as well. The decision to go to Howard held forth many promises: renewed ties with old friends, participation as an integral part of the musical life of the campus and the community, the opportunity to mold the careers of professionals, and the challenge of being part of a distinguished tradition, plus security. Hazel's appointment was part of a dream of Lulu Vere Childers, who was determined that the conservatory of music at Howard, formally established in 1914, would be one of the finest in the country. So, with practice rooms scattered all over the campus, with "never enough pianos and never enough money with which to purchase new ones," Childers, an Oberlin Conservatory graduate of 1896, set about to accomplish her dream.[3]

By 1936 Childers had assembled some of the finest talent in the country: Roy W. Tibbs, noted pianist and organist and graduate of Fisk and Oberlin, was head of the Piano Department. A familiar name to Hazel, he had performed extensively in the Midwest and on the East Coast. Another familiar name was that of Charles Cecil Cohen, also from Fisk and Oberlin. Their former classmate at Oberlin, Camille Nickerson, was also their colleague now at Howard. Madeline Coleman and Louia Vaughn Jones, who had been classmates at the New England Conservatory of Music, served as heads of the Theory and Violin departments, respectively. Baritone Todd Duncan, Howard's own Lillian Mitchell (Allen), and Gladys Rotan Chambers completed the ranks. Insisting on the very best, Childers then added the international star Hazel Harrison, pupil of Busoni and Petri.[4] "When apprised of her appointment," Lillian Allen recalled, "the faculty was elated. Her unusual talent and broad musical education would be of extreme value, and this appointment would furnish great incentive for the enrollment of new piano students."[5]

The Howard University family had already experienced the special magic of a Harrison concert when she had appeared in its concert series in 1935, playing selections by Bach and Paradies, sonatas by Schumann and Liszt, and a large Chopin group. The annual concert series had been established in 1933, with a concert by Abbie Mitchell as its first offering. It had brought a variety of musical experiences to the campus, including the National Symphony with Roy Tibbs as guest pianist. The series was a "distinct contribution to the cultural enjoyment of Washington and the Howard community."[6] The local press also promoted these concerts. Critics for Washington's major newspapers—the *Post*, the *Times*, the *Herald*, the *Star*, the *Afro-American* and the *News*

—regularly announced and reviewed major events on the Howard campus.

Hazel's first concert appearance as a faculty member was on the 1936-1937 concert series, which included the Westminster Chorus with Dorothy Maynor as soloist; Conrad Bernier, organist; Alton Jones, pianist; Frank Harrison, baritone; Hazel Harrison, pianist; Louise Burge, contralto; and Marian Anderson, contralto. Hazel's concert had received advance publicity in the local papers, which announced the program as well:

Concerto and Fugue in C Minor	Bach-Petri
Two Chorales	
"In Thee Is Joy"	Bach-Busoni
"Now Rejoice, Dear Christians"	
Fantasie in F Minor	Chopin
Scherzo in B-flat Minor	Chopin
"Confessional Song"	Beethoven-Liszt
"The Trout"	Schubert-Liszt
"Frolic of the Waters"	Ravel
Toccata	Ravel
Six Etudes after Paganini-Liszt	Busoni
Tremolo	
Andante Capriccioso	
"La Campanella"	
Arpeggio	
"La Chasse"	
Theme and Variations	

In its review, the *Post* (24 February 1937) noted the predominance of taxing transcriptions and seldom-encountered arrangements, and that Hazel's "feat of sustained bravura playing . . . deserved the enthusiastic applause which the audience expended." In very much the same vein, the *Herald* (24 February 1937) acclaimed her program as unusual, both musically and physically, concluding with the statement that "the technical feat of performing them [Paganini-Liszt Etudes by Busoni] . . . was one that commands respect."

Hazel's first campus home was in Truth Hall, where single faculty maintained rooms on the second floor and married couples were housed on the third floor. The dining room was a popular meeting place for lunch and dinner. Here, she enjoyed the camaraderie of new friends, often surprising them with homemade fudge. She performed for musical soirees in the home of President and Mrs. Mordecai Johnson. When the student body increased significantly, this dormitory was reclaimed for student residents, and the faculty had to find housing elsewhere. Lillian Allen remembered that she was the first to move to Howard Manor, an apartment house just off the campus. Hazel and others soon followed her lead, thus making for a stable community of friends and musicians.[7]

Her apartment was number 414 at 654 Girard Street, N.W. It was here that she would spend the next nineteen years. She made a home for Birdie and filled many hours practicing on a silent keyboard that she had acquired and giving extra help to students who needed it. Typically, her day would begin in the very early morning hours as she left the apartment to walk the short distance to the Conservatory to practice before her first student arrived. Allen recalled how Hazel's friends were concerned for her safety and cautioned her about walking unaccompanied in the wee hours.[8] The story circulated for years that she carried her huge handbag an ice pick or a hat pin or a butcher knife—or something. The correct version has never been established, but whatever it was, it gave her the needed sense of protection, and in all her years at Howard, she traveled safely from her apartment to her studio.

The adjustment to her new surroundings was eased by friends who invited her to dinner, to the theatre, to concerts, or for a drive. Hazel, a friendly person, readily accepted these invitations. In a letter to Gregoria Goins, Hazel acknowledges her kind gestures:

Dear Friend:
   I planned to see you today but Miss Childers had arranged for me to take a drive through beautiful Rock Creek Park and Mount Vernon, so I am writing you instead. It was so kind of you to invite me to dinner. I am working so hard trying to get adjusted. As soon as my studio is ready, I am sure I shall feel more comfortable. . . .
   Thank you for your dear letter and telephone call. . . .
   Looking forward with pleasure to Friday evening.

                                                   I remain,
                                                   Yours truly,
                                                   Hazel Harrison[9]

Hazel found herself part of a growing professional school with instructional offerings in piano, voice, other instruments, theory, and public-school music. Her studio was located in the Conservatory, which overlooked the main campus, and was flanked by Howard Hall and the Conservatory annex. These three buildings made up the School of Music complex and were strategically located around a semicircular driveway, which allowed for easy access from one building to another. As part of the Piano Department faculty, Hazel was committed to its objective: "to give a thorough foundation and . . . cultivate that musical feeling which is necessary to the development of true musicianship."[10] They guided the students through the required scales and studies for technical solidarity and a repertoire of compositions of all periods. Practice rooms were tucked into every available cranny alongside the teaching studios and classrooms.

Upon entering the Conservatory, one would be greeted with the sounds so familiar to the ears of musicians: vocalises, scales, arpeggios, a snatch of Beethoven, a measure of Bach, a few chords from Prokofiev. Frances White Hughes, well-known Washington educator, was one of Hazel's first students. She recalled their initial meeting:

I met her while walking around the driveway toward Howard Hall. She had a very jaunty step. You could tell she was pleased to be there. The manner in which she greeted me told me that this was somebody special. There was an immediate bit of chemistry seeming to happen and I knew that I wanted her to teach me.[11]

Other early students of Hazel at Howard were Robert Earl Anderson and Luis Andres Wheatley—her first graduating seniors —and several of her Tuskegee students who had followed her when she moved.

The students found in Hazel a teacher who shared from her own experiences and who taught them "how to practice." Whether it was a scale or a melodic phrase, she demonstrated her method of practicing in small fragments and the need for endless repetition. Finger independence was achieved through studies with shifts in rhythmic accents. Robert Earl Anderson, prominent Baltimore music teacher, reflected that Hazel was one of the few teachers who could and would answer his persistent questions of "why" and "how." Explaining further:

She considered me a student. This I appreciated greatly. It has meant more to me as I have gotten older, because I've been a student all my life and I'm still a student. Miss Harrison's emphasis was music. She'd show you the structure, the melodic development, and tell you why you had to play it this way. "Bring out the bass! That is the theme transposed," she'd say. And, oh! her black pencil. She was never without her big black pencil. If you did not see an accidental by a note, she'd write it in with her big black pencil. I have mended every score that she marked upon, regardless of how tattered it had become.[12]

Hazel's highly descriptive markings were considered priceless by her students. "I treasure every one of them," said Frances Hughes. Years later, when she was studying with Emerson Meyers, another prominent teacher in the area, she was admonished for not following Hazel's markings. "It's marked right there," Meyers would say. "Why don't you do it?" Hughes admitted good-naturedly that Mr. Meyers was perfectly willing to accept Hazel's interpretative markings just as they were.[13]

Hazel's students strove diligently to follow those bold markings as they practiced: "Teeter." "More brilliance." "Sing." "Whisper." "Speak loudly." Her verbal instructions were even more descriptive: "Say something, baby. Those are the same notes, so don't play them the same way twice." Or, "Now, you are the orchestra, Dolly. These are the flutes (pointing to various lines) and here are the trumpets." In another composition, she might say, "This is the bass voice—a young man talking to his lady friend and now she answers him. Change the color of your tone."[14]

It was not long before Hazel's students affectionately dubbed her "La Harrison." In their minds, she was a great pianist and one who deserved a special designation. To them, "La Harrison" said all of this. The students soon reaped the benefit of her large repertoire; they learned to love the literature of the great masters that she loved to play; they explored together the large transcriptions of Liszt and Busoni; they learned the compositions of composers who were new to them—Scriabin, Shostakovitch, and others. Not to be thwarted by their lack of technical skill, she coached her students in the necessity for an able technique. She stressed scales, octave studies, arpeggios—the tools to acquire great facility. Hughes recalled her exact words: "Once you master these techniques, your innate musicianship—whatever talent you have—will take over." "La Harrison" told them repeatedly that she expected their performances to grow in terms of depth and understanding. "Let's practice," she would say when lessons were not properly prepared. And then she would proceed to demonstrate how much one could learn in a few minutes of purposeful practice.[15]

Anderson related another of Harrison's teaching aids: "Frequently she would place her hands on top of yours. There was something electrifying about that. I don't know whether my muscular or my mental reaction did the trick. Whatever it was, it seemed to work its magic." Continuing, he remembered Hazel wore a beautiful ring of three Egyptian scarabs carved of jade. "She regarded it as her talisman—a good luck piece—the only extent I've known her to be inclined to fetish." In later years, determined to have one like it, he had one made of silver.[16]

Hermine Johnigan, a piano minor, remembers that "for me it was very exciting. I never wanted to disappoint her. I always wanted to be prepared. She had so much to give me. I spent my weekends getting music ready so that when I walked into her studio we could move ahead. It was very challenging."[17] Sterling Thomas, one of Hazel's "sons," confided that he would listen to her practice while standing outside her studio door waiting for his 7 A.M. lesson. "She would play one, two, or three measures over and over for an indeterminable length of time. Each time she would vary the accent." He added that she employed a system of weight transfer and quiet wrist playing that was peculiar to the Italian school of playing. "She wore one gold bracelet, watching it closely, to make certain that her wrist was steady and remained so."[18]

Hazel had audiences of which she was unaware. Several students who practiced late at night would stand and listen outside her door in rapt attention to those few measures that she repeated. Chester Rowlett, a violinist, confessed that upon entering the Conservatory, he would remark to himself, "That's Hazel Harrison practicing," and he would stand in awe at the sounds that filled the building. After a few minutes, he would dash to his practice room on the next floor and practice, inspired, for hours.[19]

Anderson's vivid memory of her playing reveals something of her technical ability:

Miss Harrison did not seem to have anything to deter her from doing what she wanted to do on the keyboard, and yet, she did not have what I would call a pianist's hand, if you're looking for big hands, strong fingers, and muscular playing. When she wanted the depth of the piano. she got it. Now that is something between *her* psyche and the instrument.

Continuing, he recalled that "her sound was a controlled sound, not the big sound we hear today from pianists. She would make a big sound, yet would not cause the strings to pop. Also, she could play very softly,—soft—soft, fast playing, light playing. Oh, what a thrill!"[20]

A later Howard colleague, David Stone, recalled that "she had that special talent of being able to make not-so-gifted students play like very gifted students. This was a rare gift. Aside from the success that Miss Harrison had with her own students, and sometimes I felt that she really willed them to play, so to speak, her own playing was of great interest to me." He went on to recall:

It was not a highly polished, refined kind of playing. Technically, many things seemed difficult for Miss Harrison, but she was always able to transcend the technical problems and to handle them in such a way that in the end they were resolved to contribute some expressive element to her performance. A good example was the manner in which she played the Liszt B Minor Sonata. It was an experience to hear Miss Harrison play a work like this, a rich musical experience, because beyond fingers and technique, the deep, spiritual quality which was so much a part of Miss Harrison's nature, shone through. And so her playing was deeply moving, and it was often exciting, because she was able to bring to her performance such grandeur and dignity of expression. It was very convincing. . . . She was a grand lady.[21]

The "Blue Danube" continued to be associated with Hazel. Robert Earl Anderson chuckled:

She would never teach it to me. Miss Harrison had to get it together, for often when she would begin the introduction it wouldn't hook up right. Then she would shift something and get started. And from there to the end—what a thrill it was. Now I know that there are artists who don't even play that introduction, even on recordings, and I know why.[22]

Hazel was a bit of a mystic. She spent long hours in meditation and in reading works of the great philosophers. Alfonso Harrod, now minister of Ebenezer United Methodist Church in Washington, relates that Hazel was "a student of truth with a capital T." He disclosed that "she and her mother read and studied religious science, and that Hazel practiced affirmng life in a positive sense." She chided him one time, when he was studying with her and had spoken in a negative fashion. "Oh, baby, don't do that. Always when you use 'I,' the first person, you are Somebody and you must follow that with the strongest verb you can muster." He never forgot this, nor her belief in the sustaining power of spiritual Truth.[23]

Drawing upon her own education in the Busoni salon, Hazel set about emulating the same atmosphere for her students. She established weekly class-playing sessions during which her students performed for each other, practiced stage decorum, learned the art of criticism (give and take), and broadened their repertoires while maintaining a healthy competitive spirit in the closeness of this intimate circle. She also established the annual Mother's Day recital, after which all her students gathered around the piano for a memorable photograph with her. This recital, in honor of Birdie, was subsidized from Hazel's personal funds. It was later that she was to add another dimension as a tribute to Birdie. In 1946 she initiated the Olive J. Harrison Scholarship, replenishing its funds by appearing in benefit concerts.[24] The scholarships were to be awarded to promising piano students, regardless of their ability to pay. She also assisted students in need more informally. There seemed to be a sense of knowing when a student could not buy a coat or a proper recital gown, and, more than once, she made it possible. Later, when some of them became graduate students, a letter from her would often arrive containing a ten-dollar bill, providing a new lease on life.

Hazel's teaching schedule was overcrowded. That she and Cohen carried the majority of the students in the department for several years was a summary statement by Childers in her 1938-1939 annual report.[25] In the ensuing years, Hazel averaged twenty-four students each term. She taught them twice a week individually and once a week collectively, at class-playing. Despite her crowded schedule, Hazel always found additional time to devote to her "babies," as she lovingly called them. When a student was preparing a graduating recital, it was not unusual for her to meet the student as early as 4 A.M. in the chapel in order to listen and coach.

These sessions were invaluable to the student performer, providing the opportunity to play the entire program under simulated conditions, with Hazel as the critical audience. One would wonder if the students complained. Rarely. They were indebted to her, and many of them carried over this early-morning practice habit into later life.

Warner Lawson, who succeeded Childers as dean, wrote in his 1942 annual report that "concert appearances by artist members of the faculty are a recognized means of promotion. Miss Hazel Harrison and Miss Louise Burge have made invaluable contacts in this manner which will undoubtedly have beneficial results."[26] In a subsequent report, he apprised the president of the success of Mary Wharton, one of Hazel's students who had auditioned with Olga Samaroff, distinguished pianist, teacher, and lecturer in New York. "Miss Samaroff was so impressed with her musicianship and fine talent that she offered her a scholarship for study." He pointed out further that "this distinction reflected credit upon her teacher as well as upon the work of the School."[27] Such auditions were regularly arranged by Hazel. She encouraged her talented students to pursue additional study and steered them to New York, giving them introductions to leading teachers, whom she knew well.

Despite her heavy teaching load, Hazel maintained her own level of rigorous practice, with high expectations for a full concert career. Like so many black artists, Hazel had to combine one career with another. In her case, a full-time teaching career was coupled with an extensive concert career—a feat requiring considerable stamina. Her concert schedule was formidable. When one thinks of the many hours spent in train travel, one is astounded by her endurance. She gave performances almost back to back in cities and towns up and down the East Coast, all across the South and Midwest, and into the West and Northwest. There was virtually no black college campus where she did not set her foot, and where she did not fail to leave a lasting impression. During the years between 1936 and 1940, she performed at least twice in the Howard concert series, and gave recitals at Jackson College (Mississippi), Tuskegee, Alabama State College, and Knoxville College (Tennessee).[28]

Returning to La Porte in 1938 for a concert, Hazel was reunited with old friends who extended a warm welcome at this beloved homecoming. Robert Coffeen, writing in the *La Porte Herald-Argus*, reflected that "her music isn't all that is inspirational. . . .

Other qualities which Miss Harrison possesses and which are immediately reflected to all those who come to know her are her abundant energy, her enthusiasm and her zest for all things."[29] Although it had been almost fifteen years since Hazel had been in La Porte, she recognized and greeted friends by name upon meeting them, some of whom she had not seen since she moved away in 1920. Several La Porte musicians who had studied with her in the old days "resumed" their studies with her, as she devoted a day to giving lessons to pupils who had been children and young people when she lived there. She would pass on to them her now-well-known advice, "Get a picture of every piece of music you want to play. Never let your body interfere with your mind. If a picture is in your mind, your fingers will do the work."[30]

The La Porte concert was sponsored by the Amateur Musical Club and was reviewed by Florence Andrew. Using such descriptive phrases as "rich warmth of tone," "direct sincerity of statement," "delicate tracery," "nicety of phrasing," she transmitted her deep respect for Hazel's artistry. Regarding the "Blue Danube," she wrote:

Can anyone play a waltz better than this artist, whom La Porte rightfully and proudly calls her own? We ask that, even though we know our own answer from having heard her play previously and after listening to "Arabesques on Blue Danube" by Schulz-Evler last night. What a spring tonic the first movement of this selection is, and we know of dancing hearts and buoyant spirits that were in the audience during her playing it last night.

Opening, there was the flowing first theme of the Danube—to my mind never played more perfectly than it was played last night. Then through that one to the ever-changing moods of this much-loved Strauss waltz. There is no one who can play a waltz better. If ever fingers and keys were one, it was here. It was an exhilarating performance.[31]

In a final tribute, she concluded by calling Hazel "a person of consummate musicianship," advising her readers that

the influence of her work in teaching in La Porte, . . . her majestic personality, her warm friendships, and her boundless energy which radiates from her person, can be carried on by those doing music now in this city and for those whom they are teaching, for many years to come, and Hazel Harrison's influence will go on carrying joy to others.[32]

Hazel Harrison
IN CONCERT

Presented By

The Amateur Musical Club
Thursday Evening, March 31, 1938
8:15 o'Clock

=========== PROGRAM ===========

THREE CHORALES

    Jesu, Joy of Man's Desiring ....Bach-Hess

    I Call to Thee, God ....Bach-Busoni

    Now Rejoice, Dear Christian ....Bach-Busoni

VARIATIONS ON A THEME BY BACH ....Bach-Liszt

    "Weeping, Wailing, and Complaining is the Christian's Sustenance" with a chorale at the end.

THREE PRELUDES ....Chopin

Scherzo C sharp Minor ....Chopin

ADELAIDE ....Beethoven-Liszt

Sonata after a lecture on Dante ....Liszt

1. Perpetual Motion ....Weber-Ganz

2. Intermezzo ....Brahms

3. Rhapsodie E flat ....Brahms

4. Jeux d'Eau (The Fountain) ....Ravel

5. Arabesques on Blue Danube ....Schulz-Evler

---

11. Program of the 1938 La Porte concert, sponsored by the Amateur Musical Club. *Courtesy of the Amateur Musical Club.*

It is through Florence Andrew herself that Hazel's influence is alive today in La Porte. After studying with Hazel for ten years and attending the New England Conservatory, Florence Andrew returned to La Porte in the early 1920s and opened her own studio. For over fifty years she has taught piano to the young people of La Porte, and is still actively teaching today at age eighty-five.

One of the concerts in the 1938-1939 Howard series that Hazel had a direct hand in bringing about was the appearance of her friend and mentor, Egon Petri. Two years before in Washington, he had conducted a master class and had appeared with the National Symphony Orchestra. But his appearance this time as a recitalist was a reminder to the music-loving public of the grand tradition of pianism to which he and Hazel were both heir. Like Hazel, he had gained wide popularity for his "prodigious pianism" and his "delightful personality,"[33] and his appearance at Rankin Chapel, with its fine acoustics and seating capacity of 500, was an unusual opportunity to hear him in an ideal setting.

Reviewers called attention to his arduous programming, forceful pianism, and authoritative playing. There was a single reference to heavy pedalling and lack of sensitive phrasing, but it did not dampen the generally glowing reviews. Overshadowing that one negative aspect were references to his striking dynamics, display of virtuosity, and his masterful insight. In typical Busoni manner, Petri played several encores—not the usual encore fare—but a couple of Liszt transcriptions and a pair of Chopin études.[34] Hazel remained a close friend of the Petris, and later, when she was on leave to make concert tours, she often traveled with them whenever their itineraries coincided.

Glenn Dillard Gunn, now music critic for the Washington *Times-Herald*, had periodically urged the performance of more American music and less of the European repertoire. In his column of December 19, 1940, he noted that in all the programs he had reviewed that week, performers had missed many opportunities to play music of American composers. Referring to a program that Hazel had given the night before, he observed that "Hazel Harrison was similarly unmindful of the native repertoire. Her only novelty was by the Hungarian composer, Alexander Lászlo." He spoke glowingly, however, of her playing, recalling his audience with her in earlier years:

Miss Harrison has developed into a remarkable pianist in the years that have passed since I heard her first recital in Chicago, where her career began. She has today a technical equipment that is definitely that of the virtuoso, and her gift for the pianistic address is vivid, urgent, and eloquent.

Gunn's efforts to create an awareness of American music paled beside the Herculean efforts of Harriet Gibbs Marshall to the cause of Negro music and musicians. For more than two decades, she had worked assiduously to establish a National Negro Music Center that would "aid in research and preservation of the music of [the] black heritage, would develop a library of Negro music, would present concerts, and would prepare books for use in the public schools that emphasized the black heritage in music."[35] With the talented faculty of her Washington Conservatory of Music, she mapped out courses, programs, and other events that would highlight its purpose and create funds for its support. The concerts featured the leading black artists of the day, and it is likely that Hazel was among those invited to appear. But funds were slow to come in, and the ultimate goal of $100,000 seemed far beyond grasp. Mrs. Marshall's work was interrupted in 1923, when she went to Haiti with her husband, the newly appointed cultural attaché.[36]

Ten years later, she revived her plan and, after a few years, launched a vigorous endowment-fund campaign, augmenting the Board of Trustees to include Mrs. Franklin D. Roosevelt, Walter Damrosch, Theodore Roosevelt, Jr., W. C. Handy, and the presidents of Tuskegee Institute and the Urban League. It was especially important to establish a library because "many Negro melodies have been lost through the years, and one of the purposes . . . is to establish a great library . . . where research workers may list and file manuscripts. Some of the work has been done, but much more remains."[37] Many years later, after the conservatory closed, the records, music, documents, and other effects were placed, appropriately, in the Moorland-Spingarn Research Center at Howard University, one of the major repositories for the preservation of the black heritage.[38]

Hazel's pattern of life—teaching, practicing, and performing —continued into the 1940s. There was a major concert at the

Detroit Institute of Arts during its 1941-1942 season; a special program in the Howard concert series in 1945 to obtain funds for a scholarship in memory of her mother; and in November of the same year, there was a New York concert under the auspices of the American Russian Cultural Association, consisting entirely of Russian music:

"Fairy Tale," G Major	Medtner
"Fairy Tale," B-flat Minor	
"Fairy Tale," E-flat Major	
Prelude, E Major	Rachmaninoff
"Moment Musical," E Minor	
Fantasie in F-sharp Minor, opus 28	Scriabin
Third Sonata, A Minor	Prokofiev
"Aromas de Leyenda" (manuscript)	Slonimsky
"Imperia" (manuscript)	
(From "Spanish Silhouettes")	
First Performance	
Valse	Jelobinsky
Nocturne	
Toccata	
Etude	
"Fantasie Orientale"	Balakirev

This concert was memorable, not only to Hazel, but also to several of her students: Charles Ella Elliott, Yvonne Tibbs (Hobson), Frances Hughes, Hermine Johnigan, and Mary Smith. They decided to surprise "La Harrison" by attending this concert. For weeks they had plotted and saved their money for the train trip; there was much excitement surrounding their plan. When they arrived in New York, they hurried to the concert hall on West Fifty-seventh Street. Making themselves known to the usher as students of Hazel Harrison, they were escorted to front-row seats where they would be among the first to see her, and be seen. When she made her entrance, a look of surprise flitted momentarily across her face, and then she smiled her big, warm smile and exclaimed, "Ooh, babies! Oooh, my babies! You shouldn't have! Oh, you darlings!" Then she sat down and played, giving the "Blue

Danube'' as an encore. At the reception, she proudly introduced her students, and afterward she took them to her apartment at 188 West 135th Street.

"Babies, what would you like to do now? Go to have some ice cream or go to Small's Paradise?"

"Small's Paradise? That's a night club!" said one student, wondering how *she* knew about Small's Paradise.

Looking at one another, they demurely replied, "Ice cream."

Having ice cream, or tea and sandwiches, remains to this day, for many of her former students, the proper vehicle for winding down after a performance. "La Harrison" and her charges enjoyed the rest of that Sunday evening and almost missed the last train back to Washington, They all dashed down the platform to catch the train, giggling like small children and bubbling with excitement over the events of that special day.

One of the unhappy experiences of Hazel's life took place about this time. Recognizing the need for top flight management, she went to the Hurok Concert Bureau to seek representation. She was given material to prepare for an audition with a screening committee and was told to return in two weeks. Confiding in her friend Alfonso Harrod, she spoke of taking time off to use every available moment for practice. "I was determined to do it. I wanted to play my very best." Upon her return to New York, Hurok, after hearing her play, shook his head sadly and gently informed her, "You are one of the greatest. You play like the masters and there is none other out there that plays any better. But the public is not ready to accept a Negro pianist. You are ahead of your time."[39] It was a serious blow, and she was stunned. There had been such high hopes for this liaison and for its resulting possibilities. But, never one to brood or be bitter, she began making other plans in her pursuit of a full concert career.

Hazel took a three-year leave of absence from Howard and set out on a cross-country tour. Cecil Cohen, then head of the Piano Department, reported in the 1949 annual report that "she had a most successful trans-continental tour, giving in the neighborhood of 100 recitals." The list of engagements for the month of January 1947 provides a glimpse of her rigorous schedule:

> January 15   Gastonia, North Carolina
>
> January 16   Rome, Georgia

January 17   Gadsden, Alabama

January 20   Tuscaloosa, Alabama

January 21   Jackson, Mississippi

January 22   Greenwood, Mississippi

January 23   Bostrop, Louisiana

January 24   Pine Bluff, Arkansas

January 26   Tulsa, Oklahoma

January 27   Bauskogee, Oklahoma

January 28   Chickasha, Oklahoma

January 30   Greenville, South Carolina

The February schedule was equally demanding. It included:

Austin, Texas

Temple, Texas

Fort Worth, Texas

Corpus Christi, Texas

Marshall, Texas

Alexandria, Louisiana

Houston, Texas

New Orleans, Louisiana

Atlanta, Georgia

Chattanooga, Tennessee

Winston-Salem, North Carolina[40]

Continuing her heavy schedule, Hazel played some eighty concerts in 1948, appearing in New York, Pennsylvania, Connecticut, Michigan, Ohio, Missouri, Arkansas, Louisiana, Alabama, Georgia, Texas, North Carolina, South Carolina, Florida, Mississippi, Tennessee, Virginia, West Virginia, New Mexico, Utah, Idaho, and California. Hazel retained the reviews of these concerts for use in publicity releases. The headlines alone tell the story:

October 6, 1947
Toledo Blade
HAZEL HARRISON GIVES SKILLFUL PIANO CONCERT

October 6, 1947
Toledo Times
**HAZEL HARRISON, PIANIST, AND CHICAGO
SYMPHONY QUARTET WELL RECEIVED**

October 22, 1947
McComb (Miss.) Enterprise Journal
**NOTED PIANIST ENTRANCES CROWD
AT MAGNOLIA**

[no date]
Coastal Georgian
**REVIEWER FINDS ARTIST SHOWS
"LOVE OF MUSIC"**

October 30, 1947
Magnolia (Miss.) Gazette
MACDOWELL CLUB SPONSORS PIANIST

November 8, 1947
Hickory (N.C.) Daily Record
NEGRO PIANIST MUSICAL TREAT

March 5, 1948
Las Cruces (N.M.) Sun News
**HAZEL HARRISON ACCLAIMED FOR PIANO
INTERPRETATIONS OF CLASSIC MUSIC**

March 19, 1948
El Centro, Calif. *Imperial Valley Press*
HAZEL HARRISON WELL RECEIVED IN CONCERT

April 7, 1948
Tacoma News Tribune
**MISS HARRISON DELIGHTS WITH
PIANO PLAYING**

April 22, 1948
Logan *Herald-Journal*
**HAZEL HARRISON PLAYS LOGAN CONCERT
WITH BRILLIANCE, TECHNICAL ADDRESS**

April 23, 1948
Twin Falls *Times-News*
**BUHL AUDIENCE ENJOYS PIANIST
HAZEL HARRISON**

April 24, 1948
Salt Lake Tribune
**PIANIST PLEASES AUDIENCE DURING CONCERT
IN SALT LAKE**

April 24, 1948
Salt Lake Telegram
BRILLIANT RECITAL HEARD BY FEW

April 24, 1948
Salt Lake City *Desert News*
**PIANIST GIVES SALT LAKE AUDIENCE
MUSICAL TREAT**

May 15, 1948
Cheboygan, Michigan
NEGRO ARTIST GIVES SPLENDID PERFORMANCE

May 21, 1948
Muskegon Chronicle
**WE BOW, MISS HARRISON,
BEFORE BRILLIANT ARTISTRY**

November 29, 1948
Toledo Times
INADEQUATE PIANO HAMPERS RECITAL

January 7, 1949
York Dispatch
400 ATTEND CONCERT
Hazel Harrison Pleases Near-Capacity
Audience with Sparkling Program

March 2, 1949
Port Arthur News
MASTERY OF PIANO SHOWN IN CONCERT

Climaxing the three-year tour was the concert of all concerts: an appearance in the Hollywood Bowl with the Hollywood Bowl Symphony Orchestra. This was to be the last major event at the convention of the National Association of Negro Musicians. Now in its thirtieth year, the NANM brought together some of the nation's most outstanding black artists to celebrate this anniversary. Taking place in Los Angeles in August 1949, the convention schedule followed a well-established pattern of concerts and clinics for chorus, organ, piano, voice, and church music. Recognition and promotion of young artists was undertaken in the youth division recitals, the scholarship auditions, and the resulting finals. Another feature was the emphasis on the music of black composers. That year, William Grant Still led a discussion-analysis of his opera *Troubled Island*, and Camille Nickerson, a past president of NANM, presented in a midday concert "Music of New Orleans." The honors-night concert featured the 200-voice convention chorus performing "The Singers" by John W. Work, guest conductor, and starring Helen Thigpen, soprano soloist. Jester Hairston and guest Dmitri Tiomkin lent their expertise in a panel discussion entitled "Problems of Synchronization of Choral and Orchestral Music in Motion Pictures." Using excerpts from the motion pictures "Duel in the Sun" and "Portrait of Jennie," they gave examples of scoring and techniques of reproduction.[41]

The high point of the conference was the Artist Concert, featuring Ellabelle Davis, soprano, Hazel Harrison, pianist, and Lena Horne, star of stage and screen. With Izler Solomon conducting, the program began at 8:30 P.M. before a large audience. It opened with the Beethoven "Leonore" Overture, No. 3, after which Miss Davis sang an aria from Mozart's *Magic Flute* and the "Allelulia" from his *Exsultate Jubilate*. Following this was a performance of William Grant Still's "Archaic Ritual" by the orchestra, and the aria "Ritorna Vincitor" from Verdi's *Aida* by Ellabelle Davis. Then the spotlight fell on Hazel, who walked confidently to the piano, bowed to the vast audience, sat down, and played the Grieg A Minor Piano Concerto. The concert closed with songs by Lena Horne.[42]

Back in Washington, Howard University, proud of its prominent faculty member and her latest achievement, publicized her appearance in a feature article entitled "Hazel Harrison's Triumph" in its alumni magazine. It mentioned that there had been only two rehearsals, and it continued:

> Playing before a huge Hollywood Bowl audience on a regular Hollywood Bowl concert series was a great triumph for the talented artist, for although she appeared in more than eighty concerts last season and received the enthusiastic applause of music critics and music lovers for her superb artistry, none of the concert halls in which she appeared compared in size and importance with the Hollywood Bowl.
>
> Miss Harrison, though rated by many music critics as one of the finest pianists in America today, is still relatively unknown in some sections of America.
>
> But today, she has finally begun to bask on the horizon of musical success. Her triumph in the Hollywood Bowl Concert will pave the way for many similar outstanding performances. Hazel Harrison's dream is coming true.[43]

Her leave of absence now over, Hazel returned to her teaching duties at Howard and began to prepare students for jury examinations, graduating recitals, and auditions for further study. Never one to rest on past laurels, Hazel continued her own lessons, commuting to New York at least once a month to study with Sina Fosdick, director of the Roerich Academy.[44] In a flurry of activity in 1952 and 1953, she gave a series of concerts, including in her schedule Virginia State College, a private recital at Central State College in Wilberforce, Ohio, the Roerich Foundation, a southern tour, and a Canadian tour that included Ontario, Manitoba, Saskatchewan, and Alberta. In Washington, D.C., she performed at the Lincoln Temple Church and was presented in concert at Howard by Phi Mu Alpha. The report of this event noted that "because she had not been heard by a university audience in several years, she was greeted by a large and enthusiastic audience."

Alice Eversman's account in the *Star* (23 April 1953) affirms the enthusiasm and warmth surrounding this concert:

> Hazel Harrison, pianist, made one of her infrequent appearances . . . at Howard University and was welcomed with tumultuous applause.
>
> The renowned artist . . . performed the last part of her program surrounded by the baskets of flowers sent by her admirers. Her thanks for the warm reception were expressed by Warner Lawson, dean of the music

school, who said the proceeds from the concert would go to the Olive J. Harrison Scholarship Fund. . . .

While the grand manner in performance is hers to command, Miss Harrison's technique is not always impeccable or the phrasing smooth. . . . As the program progressed, her interpretations gained in poetry and fire, although her tendency to rhythmic imbalance persisted somewhat. Yet her deeply musical nature shone through in the creation of lovely sound, at times of quite striking sweetness, and in her abandon to the influence of the music.

With Birdie now gone, Hazel more than ever felt the need for the companionship of her friends. She wrote long letters and spent many pleasurable hours in visits. She renewed old friendships. She and her favorite cousin, Frank Harrison, Jr., visited Paris together in 1952. Upon her return, she received a citation from the Music Association of Indiana for her outstanding work in concert performance.[45]

These activities resurrected her ambition for a full concert career. She believed that the time was fortuitous for concerts here and abroad. Her friends heard her say, "I must get ready. I'm going back to Europe." She also believed that Allen Moton could do much to further this idea. Promising to be her agent, he convinced her that, together, they could accomplish this. So, heart aflutter and eyes aglitter, Hazel agreed to marry Moton. Just as quickly as she had consented, she discovered that she had made a mistake; and just as quickly, she hastened to rectify it. The only reference she ever made to it was, "Tsk, tsk. Mexican divorce. Mexican divorce."[46]

In 1954, at age seventy, she was invited to perform at the National Gallery in its concert series. The *Afro-American*'s music critic, Virginia Williams, made weekly announcements of the coming event. In her December 5 (1953) column, she wrote that "Miss Hazel Harrison plays at the Mellon Art Gallery January 3, Sunday evening. Atmòsphere and Miss Harrison's fine program will give music lovers one of the most rewarding evenings the New Year can bring." On December 19 she reported, "Enthusiasm is running high in the anticipation of the unusual recital scheduled at the Mellon Art Gallery presenting Miss Hazel Harrison. This appearance is interesting friends who plan to be present from Baltimore, Md., Wilmington, Del., Philadelphia and New York."

The National Gallery concerts are one of Washington's most distinguished series. The gallery's East Garden Court, with its resplendent flora, is a popular gathering place on Sunday evenings. Lines begin forming as early as two hours before the concert, and when the guards lower the entrance ropes, there is a scramble to obtain the seats around the fountain. On the night of Hazel's performance, the audience included the regulars plus her own following. The concert was broadcast over Washington station WGMS and the Continental FM Network and was given critical review by the three major papers.

Virginia Williams, reviewing for the *Afro-American* (9 January 1954), compared Hazel to other performers: "Of all the recitalists who flourish today, there is none quite the equal of Miss Harrison. She can match them all, talent for talent, gift for gift, and when the measuring is over there is something left over that cannot be measured." She related further that the audience refused to leave, even after two encores, one of which was the "Blue Danube," until Hazel had acknowledged several curtain calls. She concluded: "Howard University has on its faculty a bevy of talented musicians. Miss Harrison has brought honor to the school repeatedly. . . . She is one of the few musicians who has never abandoned diligent daily practice; hence, she arouses large audiences to ovations every time she performs."

In sharp contrast was the *Evening Star*'s stinging review (4 January 1954) by Day Thorpe:

Miss Harrison is so delighted with the big sound she is able to coax from a grand piano that she keeps the sustaining pedal down throughout almost everything she plays. This procedure does not help her achieve an orthodox performance of Bach, but no matter, for such orthodoxy is far from her desires. Her aim is a free realization of the Busoni transcription of the famous chaconne for unaccompanied violin, a realization effected by melodic, rhythmic and dynamic waywardness that mirrors her own abandonment to the overwhelming piece.

Thorpe conceded, however, that this sound was more appropriate in the Russian compositions. "Finally," he continued,

Miss Harrison found her perfect vehicle in Liszt's variation on Bach's chromatic capriccio on the departure of his brother. . . . In this work Miss

Harrison displayed a type of unrestrained pianism one reads about but seldom hears. She should have stopped at this point. Her further efforts with the Busoni transcriptions . . . and finally the paintpot of the László . . . did nothing to show a different side of her artistry.

The *Afro-American* reviewer could not let this criticism go by without a rebuttal. In her next column (16 January 1954), she advised her readers that Thorpe, the new music critic for the *Evening Star*, had made an amusing comment about Hazel's successful concert:

Amusing because he criticised her on a number Miss Harrison did not play. She did not play Liszt's Variations on Bach's Chromatic Caprice on the departure of his brother. What Miss Harrison did play was the Bach-Liszt Weeping, Crying, Sobbing, Sighing which concluded with that marvelous chorale from the Mass in B Minor which she so masterfully performed.

Tossing off the pedalling rebuke, Williams continued:

I was proud to have been sitting less than twelve feet away from the artist and never was there overuse of the sustaining pedal. Again, Mr. Thorpe, the piano upon which she played was a good one similar to those she had used in her home, on the concert stage in America and in Europe with the same great dexterity. A grand piano is not a stranger to Miss Harrison, Day Thorpe. Rudeness is never appropriate.

Calling upon the *Star* for an apology to Miss Harrison, Williams concluded her rebuttal with a statement of the elegance, dignity, and authenticity with which Alice Eversman, the *Star*'s former music critic, had written for twenty-one years. In a final barb directed at the new critic, Williams stated that "the entire nation will miss her writings."

The third review of the concert, written by Glenn Dillard Gunn of the *Times-Herald* (4 January 1954) furnished readers with a resumé of Hazel's career and a tribute to her musicianship:

Hazel Harrison, who played Sunday night in the National Gallery of Art, is quite surely the dean of native pianists.

One must assume that she has been longer before the concert public than any of her compatriots, or, for that matter, than any European who comes to mind.

I am reasonably certain of this because I was assigned to review her debut in the first decade of the present century. I judge about 1908. This took place in Chicago. Thereafter, as student and artist she extended her activities to Europe, seeking the guidance, finally, of Ferruccio Busoni. .
She found this profitable, as did all who had contact with the towering genius.
Miss Harrison is now a dignified figure on the concert stage. She sits quietly before the piano, playing without mannerisms of any kind but with a highly developed technical command of the instrument and musical approach that is always interesting and individual.
The program that she offered on this occasion was exacting. She quoted Bach transcriptions by Siloti, Busoni and Liszt, all of which are demanding and exciting pages. The Busoni transcriptions dealt with the great Chaconne and has been a challenge to the last two generations of pianists.
The Liszt transcription was in fact a set of variations by the great Hungarian virtuoso and not a transference of Bach ideas to the piano keyboard. This, too, is a composition of notable difficulty. Between the Bach-Busoni and the Bach-Liszt Miss Harrison explored briefly the contemporary Russians, such as Medtner and Scriabin.
Both the ancient and the modern compositions were treated with sympathy and understanding and notable command of the resources of the instrument.
After the intermission Miss Harrison turned again to Busoni for the revisions of certain Paganini Caprices as set by Liszt. To close her program she quoted a contemporary Hungarian named László, who complicated his message by many detailed descriptions for color suggestions.

The "dean of native pianists" decided to draw her teaching career to a close. Amid tears and expressions of sadness, she retired in June 1954, only to return during the summer session for one more year. In typical Harrison style, she just had to see one more of her "babies"—Esther Wroten, her last piano major—through her graduating recital. Another unfinished task was the appointment of someone to the piano faculty to fill her vacancy. In Hazel's mind, there was no question as to who that person should be. She recommended to the dean that Vivian Scott, her former student, be considered to carry on her work in the Piano Department. Since graduating from Howard, Vivian's concert appearances had been well received, and her name as a promising concert pianist was growing rapidly. Vivian was appointed. Now Hazel could breathe easily, and so she made her final exit in September 1955.
Those around her reluctantly acknowledged that retirement was

the most appropriate move for Hazel. At seventy-two years of age, she was faced with mandatory retirement, a decrease in the number of students interested in concert careers, and other indications of change in the philosophy of music education and in student needs.

The entire faculty, now having grown to twenty-six, turned out to honor her at a luncheon-reception held in the university dining room. One after another, her colleagues expressed their devotion. The tenured members recalled the long years they had shared. The others, especially the younger ones to whom she had been such a great friend, took turns to greet her. At the climax of this nostalgic gathering, President and Mrs. Johnson and Dean Lawson paid her a tribute for her years of untiring service to the university and for her great cultural role to the nation and presented her with a magnificent medallion.

Hazel's plan was now to return to New York and spend the remaining years there. She busied herself with packing, sorting, discarding, and shipping materials to the New York apartment. She had collected bits and pieces from everywhere and was reluctant to part with them and the memories they generated. Just to pack her library alone was a gargantuan task. Her music holdings were priceless, and many of the editions out of print. They had come from the major publishing houses of Paris, New York, Leipzig, Mainz, the Soviet Union, Philadelphia, Boston, and Vienna. Among the editors were J. Hamelle, Edward Dannreuther, Carl Haslinger, Alfred Cortot, Lucien de Lacour, Alphonse Leduc, and A. Durand et Fils. The editions were well known to performers and musicologists: Breitkopf and Härtel, Éditions Salabert, Durand, Société de Grandes Editions Musicales, La Section Musicale des Editions d'Etat Moscow, Belaieff, and others. American editions came from Schirmer, C. F. Peters, Carl Fischer, M. M. Cole, and Associated Music. Hazel had two and three copies of the same work and studiously compared fingerings, phrasing, and other pianistic details.[47] All this music, along with programs dating back to the first part of the twentieth century, had to be boxed carefully.

Her good friend Sina Fosdick expressed concern for this chore in a letter to Hazel, saying, "I am surprised you had to do it all by yourself! Have you no pupils devoted to you or close friends who could have helped you? To pack the accumulations of many years all by yourself is indeed a terrible task, and I only hope that it has not overstrained your arm muscles.''[48] Unknown to Sina, Hazel's urgent plea for help had been answered willingly by several friends who assisted in sorting her mountain of materials.

Sina Fosdick's concern went further. Having been Hazel's coach for years, she instructed her to continue to work with scales, practicing them "with different accents, and also concentrate on the first five exercises of Clementi. You can also take the octave study from Clementi-Tausig, the one we used to do years ago, and work on it for speed, but practice it lightly, with the whole arm, not with the wrist at all." In closing, she told Hazel to call her when she was fully settled in her apartment and when she had regained her strength.[49] It would be a very good guess that Hazel needed time to rest. Her arthritis was flaring up and she was tired.

Her old friend Alfonso Harrod came to her aid at this critical time. Of great moral support, he assisted her tremendously in this transition period. He shared the apartment with Hazel and her other student, Esther Wroten, continuing his piano studies with her and performed secretarial and other chores. Esther was able to receive coaching from Hazel and to share in Hazel's life in very much the same manner that Hazel herself had participated in the Busoni household. Esther describes the apartment as having a "grand piano in the living room which she [Hazel] rarely played. This room looked very much like a parlor setting of the nineteenth century, with Tiffany lamps, overstuffed chairs, a tapestry covering the piano, and photographs around the room." Later, Esther studied with Sina Fosdick and reported her progress to Hazel frequently. She remembers that "Miss Harrison would never make any comment or give any help to me when I was studying with Sina Fosdick. She tried to avoid any friction among the three of us. She would, however, attend some of my recitals, which was very encouraging to me.''[50]

New Yorkers were happy to see Hazel again. She attended lectures and concerts and carried on long conversations with dear friends—most often with Mayme White, Gertrude Curtis, Edward Boatner, Raffaello Busoni, Charlotte Moton Hubbard, and Reginald Mitchell. And, of course, there were the inevitable piano students.

Accustomed to public performance and aware of its pitfalls, Hazel undertook the preparation of students for performance in

130   BORN TO PLAY

high-pressure situations. She circulated a letter to that effect:

Dear Student
In lieu of class playing I have decided to have Class Lessons the 2nd and 4th Sundays of each month from 1:30-5:30 P.M. These Class Lessons are designed to prepare the student for examination and to aid in any other problems he may have in performance.
The first meeting will be held Sunday, September 8, 1957 at my studio, 188 West 135th Street, Apartment 4E.
At the first meeting emphasis will be placed on entrance examinations as well as performance.
A fee of $5.00 per session will be charged.
Arrangements can be made for those desiring private lessons.

Yours truly,
Hazel Harrison[51]

Before long, however, Hazel became restless for college teaching and mentioned her availability to friends at Alabama State College. Late in 1957, she was approached by H. Councill Trenholm, president of the college, who requested a conference with her while he was in New York attending to other matters.[52] They explored the possibility of her returning to Alabama during the regular academic year, when a member of his piano faculty would be on leave. She gave it serious thought because her doctor had long been suggesting that a milder climate would be better for her arthritis. Finally, she made up her mind to go, but, before leaving, there would have to be a concert.

Esther Wroten remembers that Hazel was very nervous about this one. She doubled her practice time, and even used the grand piano, which was rare. The big night came, on June 6, 1958, at Second Canaan Baptist Church. Esther was there. "Her performance was tremendous. She truly lived up to all of the newspaper comments on the program. Among those in attendance that night was composer-arranger Hall Johnson. He was raving about her performance to me."[53]

After arranging for a friend to keep the apartment, and packing only a few things, Hazel set off for Alabama.

6

ALABAMA STATE COLLEGE: 1958–1963

Mildred Hall was surprised, one afternoon in late 1958, to look up and see Hazel Harrison standing in the doorway of her studio in DeRamus Hall, wanting to know why the studio had not been vacated and made ready for her. Since Hazel had not been very definite about her arrival, no one was sure when to expect her, and Mildred had not had time to vacate. Mildred was taken aback by Hazel's brusqueness, especially in the light of their previous pleasant pupil-coach relationship. But within a few days, Hazel had settled in, placed her "Hazel Harrison, Pianiste" sign on the studio door, and Mildred was making more concrete plans for her leave of absence.[1]

Making the change from New York to Montgomery had not been too hard for Hazel. It was only forty-odd miles from Tuskegee, where she had begun her teaching career more than twenty-five years before, and she looked forward to seeing her many friends still in the area. William Dawson had remained at Tuskegee and was still actively composing, arranging, and conducting. Mary Goldsmith, her former pupil who years before had commuted to Tuskegee to study with her, was still in Alabama State's Music Department. Portia Trenholm, also one of Hazel's commuting students from Tuskegee days, was chairman of Integrated Arts, taught appreciation courses, and was the first lady of the college. Portia Pittman, her closest friend at Tuskegee, now lived in Washington, and had been preoccupied over the past decade with the realization of her father's national monument.

Montgomery of 1958 was still caught up in the civil rights movement, although the bus boycott had been resolved. Not far from
the campus was the Dexter Avenue Baptist Church, now a mecca
for visitors. Martin Luther King, Jr., preached there on Sundays
when he was in town and when his schedule permitted. The college
had continued to grow and to expand its offerings. The name had
been changed from Alabama State College for Negroes to Alabama
State College, to reflect the times as well as its new thrust as provider
of quality education for all—from the laboratory school through
the master's degree programs. During her tenure at Howard, Hazel
had come to the college several summers at the invitation of her
friend and supporter, Frederick Hall, who was, until 1955, chairman of Alabama State's Music Department. She had given piano
workshops, presented students in recital, and provided special
coaching to advanced students. There were also her own concert
appearances at Tuskegee and at the Alabama State branch at
Mobile. It was during those summers that Hazel had come to know
Mildred Hall, now one of the luminaries of the music faculty and
well known throughout the South as a distinguished pianist and
teacher.

Overall, the Music Department was pleased to have Hazel join
them. Although now seventy-five years old, she was still musically
active and made no concessions to her arthritis, and her qualifications for teaching advanced piano were undisputed. Not everyone
felt that way. There were those within the department who felt that
Hazel was past her prime and that Alabama State did not need a
declining prima donna. Her colleague Althea Thomas felt that in
spite of this, she was accepted as the "pre-eminent authority in
pedagogy and technique. She was unquestioned. She was uncom-
monly fluent. She was very, very technically able . . . and her style
was so *far* superior."[2] This, plus her storehouse of knowledge and
great wealth of travel experience, added another raison d'etre to
her being there.

As a piano teacher, Hazel had continued to believe in the
primacy of technique. "I don't hear enough Czerny being played,"
she insisted. "I don't hear enough scales in thirds. What about
dominant seventh arpeggios?" She attended to the practice habits of
all students, no matter whose they were. The practice rooms in the
main music building were in the back, with teachers' offices along

the sides and the chairman's office up front. Often, as Hazel passed through the practice area and heard something that was wrong, she would open the door and say, "Oh, no, ba-a-by, no! Let's practice," as she would lead the student through the passage. No one was offended.[3]

Even the music faculty was not exempt. One of her young colleagues, Ralph Simpson, remembers:

One day she heard me playing. I was getting ready for a form and analysis class. We were talking about ternary form. I wanted to use one of the Arabesques by Debussy as a piece to examine. She heard me sight-reading this, and I guess she thought I was working on it to play in public.

"Baby, that's beautiful. Er, —when is your recital?"

"Well, I don't plan to—"

"Oh, no, you must play this. You must get it ready. Come, let's go and work a little bit."

So we went to her studio.

I wish something could be written about her pedagogical methods. I don't think they can be found anywhere. . . . You must know something about the piece, how the name was derived, etc. And once you begin to play, you get maybe three notes played and she would cover your hand and ask, "What do you feel?" Well, I didn't know what she was trying to get at. "What do you feel? What chord is this? Why do you think he wants more emphasis on the C? Where is the melody?" She used an analytical approach to teaching that I haven't seen used before. And it's a very slow process. It would take three sessions to read, very slowly, through one composition. But once you got through it you had memorized it. You knew where every finger belonged. . . . She would write funny expressions in the margin of compositions. In this Arabesque, the phrase kind of peaked, and she wrote, "We've reached the mountaintop!" I still have that music with some of her comments.[4]

It was this analytical approach that reached another student, Paul Gary. When he was accompanying the choir, Hazel went through all the piano scores of the choir's repertoire with him. "That was the way she was," he reflected.

She'd sit there with that little tam and that little sweater, a gray skirt, white stockings, and the shoes would not be ballet shoes, but similar to what my grandmother used to wear, with the little strap across . . . and she'd call out the chord changes. I think it was then that I learned how to really memorize music according to schemes instead of notes.[5]

Confessing his dislike for scales and for Czerny, Gary conceded to her demands in this respect, and she, recognizing his love for more dissonant harmonies, introduced him to Kabalevsky, Rachmaninoff, and other Russian composers and their compositions. "The Rachmaninoff Prelude really got me into the Rachmaninoff thing, because I am now trying to do his whole repertoire. She exposed me to a lot of music . . . and she taught me to sight read." Gary, now an art teacher in Maryland, looks back in retrospect to his affection for her and to the appreciation of great music he learned from her. "I tell my kids sometimes when we talk about black pride, 'Oh, yes, Hazel Harrison, the world's greatest black concert pianist—' They look at me like I'm from space."[6]

She even devised her own system for teaching scales to the non-piano majors. Simpson said,

Some of the guys had trouble getting the thumb under, after the third finger, so, in that instance, she would teach a "cluster" scale. This is how it went: let the thumb in the right hand, for instance, play C, then let the second and third fingers play D and E at the same time, then put the thumb under—and she insisted on letting the wrist rotate and the elbow raise—and then play fingers two, three, and four in a cluster—G, A, and B. And so on up for two and three octaves. And it worked. "You've got to know keyboard geography," she said. "Once they learn where the thumb goes, they'll play the scales." And this is so true.[7]

In another encounter with Ralph Simpson, Hazel discovered that he was a composer. As Simpson relates it,

Miss Harrison walked over into my studio, without inquiring what I was doing, and said, "Oh, baby, you are a composer!" She just anointed me a composer. "You must write something for me." She didn't wait for me to explain that I was not composing, I was just copying an arrangement. So she left and went immediately to her studio. Well, that was kind of a challenge to me. I'd done some composing, but never anything for piano. And I thought and thought, and said to myself, "What an honor it is to have such a great person as Hazel Harrison ask little me to compose something for her, and at just that moment I was convinced that I must do something for Miss Harrison. I thought, "What would you write for someone like Miss Harrison? She's played Brahms, she's played Rachmaninoff, she's played—" What would you do? Then something said to me, "What would a person in her stage of life have on her mind?" And the words "Heaven, heaven" came to me. There's that spiritual, "I got shoes, you got shoes, all

God's chillun got shoes.'' I'll use some of that in my composition. To make a long story short, I wrote the composition and dedicated it to Miss Harrison, and the title of it is "Presentiment," which means a foreboding of something to come. Miss Harrison . . . honored me by giving it its world premiere.[8]

Hazel continued to maintain the schedule that had served her so well in past years. The night watchman would escort her from her lodgings just off campus to her studio. But she had added something to her routine: she did not want anyone to hear her practicing. The moment she heard anyone around she would change the rhythm so the passage could not be identified, or else she would repeat a little motif with different accents to camouflage it. Ralph Simpson never heard his "Presentiment" in rehearsal. She would sit at a piano and ask him, "Is this the way you want this little part? OK, OK, I'm working on it." He heard the entire composition played for the first time at its premiere.[9]

The occasion was her first public appearance since arriving in Montgomery. It was part of the college's celebration of Negro History Week in 1959. Taking place on a February afternoon, the concert promised to be a pleasant enough way to spend a late winter's afternoon. There was no way of foreseeing that it would turn out to be an occasion so memorable that it is still talked about in Montgomery. Hazel's Music Department colleagues had never heard anything coming from her studio, and they expected that it would be ordinary piano playing, slow tempi, and so on. But when Hazel came onstage, she was transformed, walking out as if she were a queen. When she struck the first chord, an electricity filled the air and remained for the rest of the evening. Simpson recalls, "It was brilliant! It was fiery! Every note seemed like a pearl on a string. You could hear every note, and when it was fortissimo, it was *fortissimo!*"[10] His "Presentiment" was also a great success that evening, receiving a fine ovation. The reviewer for the Montgomery *Advertiser* (10 February 1959) deemed it to be "well worth the investigation of pianists in search of fresh recital material." It was a great evening for both the pianist and the piece. After that, Hazel was a goddess on campus. Even the football players, seeing her walking across the campus, would say something like, "Man, there's that piano lady. She wore that piano *out!*"[11]

Hazel's pupils were her family. Many of them cherish mementos that she gave them: a pin, a hat, and, of course, the markings on their music. All her students were special, no matter what their talents. Their growth was her total concern, and after study with her, they knew that they had grown. Continuing her concern, she reestablished the Olive J. Harrison Scholarship on the Alabama State campus. In addition, she continued the custom of having her students wind down after a recital by having tea and sandwiches. "You can't go home, baby. You can't go home now. You played beautifully. Stay and have some tea and let's talk about it."[12] At student recitals, she would sit in the line of vision and within earshot of the performer, and if necessary, she would call out, "Oh, baby, a little more F-sharp!" Or, "Oh, baby, too much pedal!" "Too fast, baby!" If things were going well, she would just sit and nod her head in approval.[13]

Sometimes, this "total concern" interfered with her students' social life. More than once, when she saw one of her promising "pianistes" holding hands with a young man on the campus, she would think nothing of telling him to let his friend go so that she could practice.[14] Even her older students, many of whom were teachers in the Montgomery schools with family responsibilities, fell under her allegiance to the practice muse. Their lessons were scheduled in late afternoon and, as often as not, continued far past the allotted time. When they might suggest that they had to leave, she would respond, "Oh? You have to fix dinner? Just open some cans. It won't matter."[15] She would always say, "You must be dedicated. The piano is a selfish instrument. It demands so much of you."[16] Invariably, she would follow this with her favorite quotation, "Trifles make perfection, and perfection is no trifle." Elizabeth Foster remembers this quotation and another one of her sayings that motivated her, "Practice, practice, and pray," as well as the advice, "Be a virtuoso. Don't be like the thousands of people who sit down to the keyboard. Be a virtuoso."[17]

The fastidiousness of her devotion to the muses was not carried over into certain other areas of academia. Hazel was reluctant to take the time to attend faculty meetings, insisting that she had to practice. She was indifferent to administration requests for information to update her file, which was important at this time because the college was in the throes of an administrative change. President Trenholm had been succeeded by Levi Watkins in 1962. The first objective of the new administration was the attainment of Class A accreditation for the school. From Hazel they wanted to know: What were her degrees? "Oh, I don't have any. I've got some kind of diploma but I couldn't tell you what it is." What was her date of birth? "Year one. I don't have time to keep up with birthdays."[18] Questions, questions, questions. "The new president is a pain in the neck," she wrote to Portia Pittman.[19]

While Hazel had no serious thought of retiring, she now found a situation developing in which she would have no choice. The signal was clear: retire or be fired. Clearly, the feeling was that she was too old to be of service. During this final year of teaching, word had circulated that she was to receive special recognition at a forthcoming convocation: she was to receive an honorary degree. The day of the ceremony came and all her students and faculty friends were there in expectation, but no special recognition was accorded Hazel. She broke down and cried in disappointment. It was the only time that people had seen her lose control.[20] Not even the Hurok episode had affected her so.

So, in 1963, at age 80, Hazel retired from Alabama State College and moved across town to lodgings on Cleveland Avenue in the home of a friend. She continued to give private lessons, although her facilities were cramped and her arthritis was more severe. She still traveled back and forth to New York and Washington and spent Christmas and other holidays with relatives in La Grange, Georgia.

Contrary to Busoni's admonition to her that appreciation is rare in human nature, many persons were solicitous of her comfort. They took her shopping or to the post office or simply riding around, which she loved. She continued to got to the beauty parlor and visit afterward with Mrs. Chambliss, her beautician. People knew that she liked perfume and elegant soaps, and they remembered her on special occasions or on drop-in visits. She still carried the familiar huge handbag, which by now contained fruit, medicine, and astrological forecasts, as well as the usual large roll of money. When shopping, she would hand the bag to her driver and direct him or her to retrieve whatever she needed. Her sense of humor was intact. She was often invited to dinner, after which her hostess might say, "Won't you please play a number for us, Miss Harrison?" Complying graciously, she would play the Rachmaninoff C-sharp Minor Prelude, verbalizing under her breath with the first three notes, "OH, MY GOD!"[21]

She continued to go to concerts and was pleased to know that the outside musical world still remembered her. Robert MacDonald, pianist, appearing in concert at Alabama State in March 1964, inscribed her program, "To Mrs. Harrison, *Ich freue mich, das sie gekommen sind! Alles gute* and very best wishes to you always."

Not too long before Hazel retired, an extraordinarily talented young man of about twelve years, Benjamin Ward, was referred to her. After auditioning with her, he was immediately accepted as an Olive J. Harrison Scholarship student. At first his lessons took place in her campus studio; after she moved, at his parents' home. A lesson might continue for two or three hours, always followed by his mother's bringing in sherbert and Hazel's favorite cake. Afterward, they would all listen to recordings, with Hazel making comments from time to time. Occasionally, she would play something herself. Looking at her hands and then at his, she would shake her head and say in jest, "Oh, baby, baby, your hands are so skinny." Ward says, "I always had very long, slender hands, but they were never particularly well developed or muscular. Hers were. We were virtually inseparable. Sort of an odd couple in that regard."[22]

Ward had great talent, and Hazel had visions for his future, just as Heinze had had for hers, years before. Commenting on Hazel's expectations for him, Ward says:

She was a little bit unhappy, frankly, that I had other interests. She had the idea that I should devote my exclusive attention to the piano. I never really saw myself as becoming a professional pianist the way she had been, or a piano teacher, or anything of the sort. I was quite serious about the instrument, but I think her hopes for me were not altogether consistent with my own aspirations. There wasn't any real problem. There wasn't tension between us as a result of that, but she often would speak of the occasion when I would make my orchestral debut, and she would say, "I want you to play in the White House," and that kind of thing. These were just fantasies. They were not things that I particularly wanted to do, or felt that I had an obligation to do, but they were things she mentioned incessantly. I did nothing to discourage her in that regard. I learned several concertos and played in settings that she found particularly congenial and happy. I think that she had very, very high expectations. I'm not altogether sure they were well founded.[23]

While his vision of himself may have been limited, hers was great, for she recognized his talent and nurtured it. Wendell Whalum, a protégé of Kemper Harreld at Morehouse College, expressed his appreciation when he inscribed a glee club program for which Ward had been accompanist, "To a great musician, Hazel Harrison, who holds a torch of music high. Thanks for your gifts to Benjamin Ward, Jr."

The move to Cleveland Avenue had not been too happy for Hazel. She felt very restricted in her two rooms—one containing her personal effects, the other, an enclosed porch where she had placed her small piano and all her music. Living in someone else's home hemmed her in. The most severe curtailment was that of her early morning practice. But there were other things, too. Minnie Scott, one of her postgraduate students, found that she could not bear to continue to study with Hazel in her new surroundings:

I'll be frank: I was very depressed. The last two lessons that I had were on Cleveland, where she had moved, and when she showed me all of those things in that one little corner it just really did something to me and I didn't go back. I didn't want to go back, because I wanted to remember her as I had been with her on the college campus, in DeRamus Hall where we had studied. The day that I had that lesson with her I was really very depressed. I remember they had a soap opera on and she trying to practice, and I remember that did something to me. She was trying to tell them to close the door—whoever was watching TV—it disturbed her very much. She was trying to give me a lesson, and after it was over she wanted to practice. She said, "Oh, baby, I don't have any space and I'm just really very miserable, and I can't practice. I wish I could go somewhere else." And that depressed me. I could *not* go back. There is still a question mark in my mind as to what her last words were, what happened in the end? I really wanted to go back. It seemed like such a *terrible* way to end such a *beautiful* life—to have to go to that back porch with that screen and all of her things crammed up, the piano in a little corner and that dummy clavier in that bedroom with a whole lot of other stuff. It just seemed like it should have all been out somewhere in a great big, pretty studio, with chandeliers and all of that—that's the way I pictured it. It really hurt me. I could *not* go back over there. She kept saying—I don't remember what she was charging me—"I could charge you less." And I said, "That's not it. I will try to come back." But I couldn't go back. I just couldn't.[24]

Hazel's plan to return to New York was thwarted when her good friend who was keeping the apartment died. She sent flowers because she could not attend the funeral. It was a time of loneliness and confusion. Now lacking a companion for the life she planned to resume, she agreed to go live with relatives in nearby La Grange, Georgia: Dora and Frank Harrison and Frank, Jr., with whom she had been close since early Howard days. The day Frank, Jr., came for her was traumatic. Her student Elizabeth Foster had spent the greater part of that day helping her get her things together. She wanted to go; she didn't want to go. Even after Frank arrived to take her to La Grange, he spent a great deal of time trying to help her make up her mind. He pointed out the rightness of the move. Finally she decided. She would go. She would go.[25]

7

THE FINAL YEARS

Frank Harrison was exactly Hazel's age, and his wife was a few years younger. They lived alone in the large, comfortable bungalow that their children had grown up in and left years before. Hazel's moving in was accomplished easily enough and caused no disturbance in the existing physical arrangements at 405 Hamilton Street. It was perhaps the idea itself that was flawed from the beginning. She missed having pupils and the comfort of her friends in Montgomery, and she wrote them often asking how they were, and their children, and mutual friends, and how things were at the college. She asked for pictures and continued to instruct her pupils in her letters. Her first Christmas away she wrote to Elizabeth Foster:

Dear dear one
We did have wonderful days. I can see your car drive up across the street. . . . Please do not forget the fine points. Remember your rests, especially on the Rachmaninoff. Oh, baby, I miss you so!!

Your present is gorgeous. You know my weak point. The container is beautiful. "Intimate" is so intriguing. I have it before me. I am writing for more news. Dr. Allman and Allman came by last night. Benjamin Ward has won a scholarship to study in Europe next year. I suppose you know it by this time. I just received word this morning. Oh Dolly thank you again and again for being you and that beautiful present. Love, dear one.

H L H[1]

Dear One
Think of the joy when I opened that envelope with the Baby. Both looking so beautiful! Dolly, how lovely you look with the *tall hat* and the

Baby!! How he has grown and standing. . . . Thank you dear one. Hasn't the baby grown goodlooking. Has the Superintendent by any chance heard you play? I still pray for your chance to come. I know your paths will cross. Be sure to keep your little finger outstretched & raise it. . . . Love to all my dear students. I love and remember every one. I have lost quite a bit of weight. You look grand. Remember our lunches? *Dear, dear* one. How you managed to drive and handle him too. Wonderful. Remember the Rachmaninoff & of all things the *rests*. You know the *marks. You pay attention to the rests.* Here I go teaching again. . . .

> *Your friend & teacher*
> *H. Harrison*[2]

I am not satisfied but have some great plans. The food is *good*.

Her time in La Grange was spent as her time had always been spent—practicing. While there, she gave a benefit performance for the Maidee Smith Memorial Nursery and played the "Blue Danube" on a program sponsored by the Warren Temple Methodist Church. Later, she went to Atlanta to attend a recital. Benjamin Ward, now a student at Morehouse, met her at the station.

The recital was scheduled for four in the afternoon—it was a Sunday afternoon. She arrived at perhaps twelve or one and there was a rehearsal in Sisters Chapel on the Spelman campus. Conducting, of course, at that time was Willis Lawrence James, who was a friend of Hazel's as well, voice instructor, and head of the Music Department at Spelman College. I will never forget. He was in the middle of the rehearsal. He did not know she was coming. I remember the extraordinary way in which they greeted each other. They had not seen each other in quite a long time. He stopped in rehearsal, right there in mid-phrase, and talked to the chorus—I would think none of whom had ever heard of her—about this remarkable woman. She spoke to the chorus herself briefly, and when we left I guess the rehearsal continued. That was a moment of particular poignancy, when two people who have known each other for many years but who had not been in close contact for some time—or any contact at all for some time—have suddenly and quite happily reunited. I felt great pride in having some small part in bringing them together.[3]

In La Grange, Hazel was becoming more and more unhappy. It was not her kind of environment. She was beginning to require the kind of attention that the Harrisons were not able to give her, and she rejected the idea of moving into a new nursing home that would shortly be available. She was making her own plans for her return to Washington, and wrote Reva Allman that "if things go along I shall return to Washington. My students Mr. and Mrs. Harrod have offered their home. Can *practice* and *teach* as long as I want and the students can enter from the basement side. No steps. It will take a little time to work it out. . . . Washington is best for me.!"[4]

Buoyed by the expectation of returning to Washington, Hazel began packing her belongings and making plans to have them shipped. She spent days sorting articles that she wanted to be sent to Dorothy Porter, curator of the Moorland-Spingarn Collection at Howard. When those matters were disposed of, Frank, Jr., accompanied her to Washington and saw her settled comfortably with Reverend Harrod and his wife, Nannie. It seemed a good arrangement. From time to time, she performed at the Harrods' home and taught a few private students. But paramount in her mind was the idea that she would play again, that she *had* to play. "Baby, I must practice because I must be ready. I'm not ready yet. I must practice."

She remained in touch with Benjamin Ward. During his last year in college, he was scheduled to give a recital at Atlanta's High Museum, sponsored by the Alliance Française and the Italian Cultural Society. The recital had received quite a bit of publicity, and her name had been associated with it as his instructor. Although she really was not well enough to attend, Hazel kept alive the possibility that she might actually be able to make the trip. She had discussed the program with him, and they had worked on several of the pieces together. "It was sort of my dream that somehow it would be possible for her to make that trip," Ward recalls.

We spoke by phone virtually every day, sometimes two and three times a day the week before the concert. Finally, it did become clear, the day before, that she was not physically able to make the trip. She sent me a very moving telegram that day, and then we spoke by phone the day of the concert. She said—I'll never forget—"Consider that your chest has been rubbed." She would always rub my chest before or after a performance. That was her way of communicating her special gift, her special hope for me. I'm sure that she did this with her other students as well. But that was the last thing she said before that big concert: "Consider that your chest has been rubbed." And she told me to think about that just before I went on the stage.[5]

The late 1960s in Washington were very disruptive, and Hazel found herself increasingly isolated because of her own physical condition as well as the confusing and frightening events then taking place. Now she needed a cane to get about. On one occasion, when William Dawson, now retired, came to Washington, Hazel and Portia Pittman joined him at dinner and discussed old Tuskegee times. "Hazel could hardly walk, poor thing," remembered Portia.[6] Probably a desperate need for someone close prompted her to telephone her old friend Reva Allman at Alabama State one day in the spring of 1968, asking her to come to Washington that weekend. Reva got herself together quickly and drove to Nashville, where she picked up her daughter Marian—once a star pupil of Hazel's and then a student at Meharry Medical College—and continued the drive to Washington. They talked for a while. It was almost Hazel's birthday, and Hazel played for them. Then they had to go, and, saying goodbye, they returned to Alabama.[7]

Hazel spent her time—when she was not practicing—in writing to old friends. In her letters, she interspersed bits of advice along with news of herself. "Cross your legs in public, dear." "Stretch a lot." "Don't eat any cream soups before the concert." "Scratch the dog's ears for me." She wrote to Florence Andrew: "Practice from the shoulder. For a long time I have gradually realized all power comes from the shoulder. Weight. Let it flow thru you." Further in the letter she said, "I have a wig!! Ha, ha. Have decided to live on and on. Anything is possible."[8] She always asked for snapshots.

Hazel was a member of the Harrod family, and they did much to ease the burden of her last years. Even when the Harrods took a trip to the Virgin Islands in 1969, Hazel, then eighty-five, went with them. While there, she fell, but she tossed it off lightly, saying, "Oh, I'm fine." But after they returned home, the Harrods knew something was wrong: she wasn't practicing as usual! And her health declined rapidly. They cared for her until she needed professional attention, when they placed her in Ruth's Personal Care Home. After a short time, on April 28, 1969, it was all over.

When the telegram came from Harrod telling him of Hazel's death, Benjamin Ward, by then a graduate student at Yale University, dropped everything to go to Washington. Joining with Hazel's friends and students in a silent memorial at the funeral home, he and Mary Lacey Moore offered a musical tribute to a beloved teacher. The next day the funeral service was held at Rankin Chapel on the Howard campus. Ward recalled: "At one point there was a special kind of meditation and I played a Bach chorale prelude on the organ." Tributes from her colleagues, friends, and students highlighted the loss that each felt, but it was Portia Pittman who said it best for all. She spoke without notes. She needed no written reminders, for she spoke from the heart of friendship when she said, "The end of my world has come."[9] In the silence that followed, each person there offered in his own thoughts a personal tribute to Hazel Harrison, a true friend.

Hazel was buried on a hillside at Lincoln Memorial Cemetery, holding music in her hands.

POSTLUDE

Hazel Harrison was a unique combination of musical and personal qualities. Her warmth, her rare musical gifts, and the inner force that emanated from her were fired in a crucible of time and place and experience to produce a star of the first magnitude.

Concert audiences always knew that they were in an extraordinary presence, even if they were not able to define it. Students held her in awe, as someone whose expectations must be lived up to, because she held herself to a more distant vision. This vision was reflected in her deep personal commitment to music, which sustained her all her life. Her spiritual and intellectual force was transmitted to all whom she touched, and her mission was clear to all who heard her: she was born to play.

CHRONOLOGY

Major events in the life and career of Hazel Harrison

1883   Born, La Porte, Indiana
1902   Completes high school
1904   Soloist with Berlin Philharmonic Orchestra
1911   Returns to Germany for concert tour
1912   Begins studies with Busoni
1914   Returns to the United States at outbreak of World War I
1926   Returns to Europe for additional study
1929   Honored in ceremony at University of Chicago
1930   Makes Town Hall debut
1931   Begins teaching career; goes to Tuskegee Institute
1932   Soloist with Minneapolis Symphony Orchestra
1936   Goes to Howard University to teach
1947   Granted three-year leave of absence for concert tours
1949   Soloist with Hollywood Bowl Symphony Orchestra
1954   Gives recital at National Gallery of Art
1955   Retires from Howard University
1958   Goes to Alabama State College to teach
1959   Gives last public concert
1963   Retires from Alabama State; teaches privately
1965   Goes to live in La Grange, Georgia
1967   Returns to Washington, D.C.
1969   Dies after brief illness

APPENDIX B

HAZEL HARRISON AND SELECTED MUSICIANS OF HER ERA

Timeline scale: 1850 1860 1870 1880 1890 1900 1910 1920 1930 1940 1950 1960 1970 1980

1852 ANDREI SCHULZ-EVLER, Polish pianist 1905
1862 CLAUDE DEBUSSY, French composer 1918
1863 ALEXANDER SILOTI, Russian pianist
1864 ALEXANDER GRETCHANINOV, Russian composer 1956
1866 HENRY (HARRY) THACKER BURLEIGH, Afro-American baritone 1949
1866 FERRUCCIO BUSONI, Italian-German pianist-composer 1924
1866 AUGUST SCHARRER, German composer-conductor 1936
1868 VASSILY SAPELNIKOV, Russian pianist 1941
1870 LEOPOLD GODOWSKY, Polish-American pianist 1938
1872 ALEXANDER SCRIABIN, Russian composer 1915
1873 SERGEI RACHMANINOFF, Russian composer-pianist 1943
1873 MAX REGER, German composer 1916
1874 ARNOLD SCHÖNBERG, Austrian composer 1951
1874 SERGEI KOUSSEVITZKY, Russian conductor 1951
1875 SAMUEL COLERIDGE-TAYLOR, Anglo-African composer 1912
1875 MAURICE RAVEL, French composer 1937
1877 SERGEI BORTKIEWICZ, Russian pianist-composer 1952
1878 OSSIP GABRILOWITSCH, Russian pianist 1936
1880 NIKOLAI MEDTNER, Russian composer 1951
1880 CLARENCE CAMERON WHITE, Afro-American violinist-composer 1960
1881 EGON PETRI, Dutch pianist 1962
1882 KAROL SZYMANOWSKI, Polish composer 1937
1882 ZOLTAN KODALY, Hungarian composer 1967
1882 ROBERT NATHANIEL DETT, Afro-American composer 1943
* 1883 HAZEL LUCILE HARRISON, Afro-American pianist 1969
1883 ANTON WEBERN, Austrian composer 1945
1884 ABBIE MITCHELL, Afro-American soprano 1960
1884 CHARLES TOMLINSON GRIFFES, American composer 1920
1884 WILLIAM KEMPER HARRELD, Afro-American violinist-impresario 1972
1885 ALBAN BERG, Austrian composer 1935
1886 CARL ROSSINI DITON, Afro-American pianist 1969
1887 ARTHUR RUBINSTEIN, Polish-American pianist 1982
1887 ROLAND HAYES, Afro-American tenor 1976
1890 DAME MYRA HESS, English pianist 1965
1891 SERGEI PROKOFIEV, Russian composer 1953
1893 HELEN HAGAN, Afro-American pianist 1964
1894 NICOLAS SLONIMSKY, Russian-American musicologist
1895 PAUL HINDEMITH, German-American composer 1963
1895 ALEXANDER LASZLO, Hungarian composer
1895 WILLIAM GRANT STILL, Afro-American composer 1978
1898 PAUL ROBESON, Afro-American bass 1976
1899 WILLIAM LEVI DAWSON, Afro-American composer
1900 AARON COPLAND, American composer
1901 JOHN WESLEY WORK, JR., Afro-American composer 1967
1902 MARIAN ANDERSON, Afro-American contralto
1903 RUDOLPH SERKIN, Austrian pianist
1903 TODD DUNCAN, Afro-American baritone
1904 VLADIMIR HOROWITZ, Russian pianist
1904 DMITRI KABALEVSKY, Russian composer
1906 DMITRI SHOSTAKOVITCH, Russian composer 1975

NAMES	DATES
Anderson, Marian	1902-
Berg, Alban	1885-1935
Bortkiewicz, Sergei	1877-1952
Burleigh, Henry (Harry) Thacker	1866-1949
Busoni, Ferruccio	1866-1924
Coleridge-Taylor, Samuel	1875-1912
Copland, Aaron	1900-
Dawson, William Levi	1899-
Debussy, Claude	1862-1918
Dett, Robert Nathaniel	1882-1943
Diton, Carl Rossini	1886-1969
Duncan, Todd	1903-
Gabrilowitsch, Ossip	1878-1936
Godowsky, Leopold	1870-1938
Gretchaninov, Alexander	1864-1956
Griffes, Charles Tomlinson	1884-1920
Hagan, Helen	1893-1964
Harreld, William Kemper	1884-1972
Harrison, Hazel Lucile	1883-1969
Hayes, Roland	1887-1976
Hess, Dame Myra	1890-1965
Hindemith, Paul	1895-1963
Horowitz, Vladimir	1904-
Kabalevsky, Dmitri	1904-
Kodály, Zoltán	1882-1967
Koussevitzky, Sergei	1874-1951
László, Alexander	1895-
Medtner, Nikolai	1880-1951
Mitchell, Abbie	1884-1960
Petri, Egon	1881-1962
Prokofiev, Sergei	1891-1953
Rachmaninoff, Sergei	1873-1943
Ravel, Maurice	1875-1937
Reger, Max	1873-1916
Robeson, Paul	1898-1976
Rubinstein, Arthur	1887-1982
Sapelnikov, Vassily	1868-1941
Scharrer, August	1866-1936
Schönberg, Arnold	1874-1951
Schulz-Evler, Andrei	1852-1905
Scriabin, Alexander	1872-1915
Serkin, Rudolph	1903-
Shostakovitch, Dmitri	1906-1975
Siloti, Alexander	1863-1945
Slonimsky, Nicolas	1894-
Still, William Grant	1895-1978
Szymanowski, Karol	1882-1937
Webern, Anton	1883-1945
White, Clarence Cameron	1880-1960
Work, John Wesley, Jr.	1901-1967

PROGRAM

I

Sonata in D, for 2-Pianos, K. 448   WOLFGANG A. MOZART
(1756-1791)

First movement — Allegro con spirito
Raymond Jackson and Clyde Parker

II

Etude pour les arpèges composés   CLAUDE DEBUSSY
Etude pour les huit doigts   (1862-1918)
Reflets dans l'eau
L'Isle joyeuse

Charles Timbrell

III

Six Waltzes, for Piano, 4-Hands   JOHANNES BRAHMS
(1833-1897)

Sonata for Piano Duo   RUSSELL WOOLLEN
(b. 1923)

Constance Hobson* and Hortense Kerr

INTERMISSION

IV

††Rhapsody in Blue   GEORGE GERSHWIN
(Arr. for 2-Pianos, 8-Hands*)   (1898-1937)

Raymond Jackson*, Clyde Parker
Charles Timbrell, Ronald Tymus†

V

Hazel Harrison — A Touch of Nostalgia

Acknowledgements   DR. DORIS E. McGINTY
Chairman, Department of Music

Rhapsody in E, Opus 1, No. 3 (1912)   CARL DITON**
(1886-1962)
(Dedicated, by the composer, to Hazel Harrison)

By the Beautiful Blue Danube (Excerpts)   SCHULZ-EVLER
(Concert Arabesques on Motifs by Johann Strauss)

Raymond Jackson

---

  * Former student of Hazel Harrison
 ** Black composer
  † Guest pianist
†† Permission granted by Warner Brothers Publication, Inc.

At the request of the artists NO recordings or taking of photographs during the performance will be permitted.

12. A program of piano music commemorating the birthday centennial of Hazel Harrison. Presented on February 6, 1983, at Howard University.

NOTES

CHAPTER 1

1. Shirley M. Kramer to editor, *La Porte Herald-Argus* [1980].
2. Certificate of birth, La Porte County Health Department.
3. "Information Received from Gene McDonald," mimeographed, (La Porte, Ind.: La Porte Historical Society, 1975), 1 p.
4. Interview with Frances Sampson Mask, former resident at 1306 Clay Street, November 1980.
5. Ibid.
6. Handwritten notes for a biographical sketch. Hazel Harrison Papers, Manuscript Division, Moorland-Spingarn Research Center, Howard University.
7. *La Porte Daily Herald*, 7 January 1897.
8. Ibid., 27 December 1897.
9. Interview with Althea Thomas, June 1980.
10. *Daily Herald*, 7 June 1902.
11. Ibid., 19 June, 16 July 1897.
12. Handwritten notes for a biographical sketch. Hazel Harrison Papers.
13. Interview with Alfonso Harrod, May 1980.
14. *Daily Herald*, 16 June 1898.
15. Ibid., 3 February 1902.
16. Ibid., 1 March 1902.
17. Ibid., 14 May 1902.
18. Ibid., 7 June 1902.
19. Ibid., 9 June 1902.
20. Ibid., 13 June 1902.
21. Interview with Florence Andrew, May 1980.
22. Ibid.

23. Ibid.

24. *Daily Herald*, 4 March 1904.

25. Arthur Abell, "Berlin," *Musical Courier*, 11 May 1904, p. 5.

26. Ibid., 31 August 1904, p. 7.

27. Ibid., 9 March 1904, p. 6.

28. Ibid., 3 February 1904, p. 6.

29. Ibid., 10 February 1904, p. 5.

30. Ibid., 31 August 1904, p. 6.

31. *Daily Herald*, 24 May 1904.

32. Ibid., 4 May 1904.

33. Ibid.

34. Ibid., 24 May 1904.

35. Abell, "Berlin," *Musical Courier*, 27 January 1904, p. 5.

36. Ibid., 11 May 1904, p. 5.

37. Arthur Rubinstein, *My Young Years* (New York: W. W. Norton and Co., 1971), p. 30.

38. *Musical Courier*, 17 February 1904, p. 6.

39. Rubinstein, p. 30.

40. *Musical Courier*, 10 February 1904, p. 6.

41. Rubinstein, plate opp. p. 208.

42. Ibid., p. 31.

43. Abell, "Berlin," *Musical Courier*, 9 November 1904, p. 7.

44. *Fisk University News*, October 1911, p. 56.

45. Excerpted in *Musical Courier*, 30 November 1904, p. 19.

46. Ibid.

47. Ibid.

48. Ibid.

49. Ibid.

50. *Daily Herald*, 15 November 1904.

51. Abell, "Berlin," *Musical Courier*, 9 November 1904, p. 6.

52. Roy L. Hill, *Booker T's Child* (Newark: McDaniel Press, 1974), p. 41.

53. *Daily Herald*, 26 March 1906.

54. Ibid., 14 December 1904.

55. Ibid., 21 September 1911.

CHAPTER 2

1. Arthur Abell, "Berlin," *Musical Courier*, 27 March, p. 6; 6 December, p. 5; 20 December, p. 6, 1911.

2. H. O. Osgood, "Music in Munich," *Musical Courier*, 6 September, p. 14; 11 October, p. 38, 1911.

3. Ibid., 1 November 1911, p. 38.

4. Lolita D. Mason, "Vienna," *Musical Courier*, 12 July 1911, p. 7.

5. Phillip C. Gates, "Vienna," *Musical Courier*, 8 November 1911, p. 18.

6. "Europe," *Musical Courier*, 28 February 1912, p. 20.

7. Annette K. DeVries, "Chicago," *Musical Courier*, 15 November 1911, pp. 42-43.

8. Abell, "Berlin," *Musical Courier*, 13 December 1911, p. 6.

9. Ibid., 17 April 1912, p. 7.

10. Rene DeVries, "Chicago," *Musical Courier*, 24 April 1912, p. 46.

11. *Musical Courier*, 15 May 1912, p. 7.

12. *Crisis*, December 1912, p. 67.

13. Harold C. Schonberg, *The Great Pianists* (New York: Simon and Schuster, 1963), p. 351.

14. "Busoni in Chicago and St. Louis," *Musical Courier*, 1 February 1911, p. 28.

15. Ibid.

16. Interview with Alfonso Harrod, May 1980.

17. Edward J. Dent, "Ferruccio Busoni," in *International Cyclopedia of Music and Musicians*, 10th ed. (New York: Dodd, Mead and Co., 1975), p. 320.

18. Reva W. Allman, "A Pianist of Distinction." Brochure prepared for Beta Nu Omega Chapter of Alpha Kappa Alpha Sorority, Inc. [ca. 1965].

19. "Victor Heinze to Tour in Germany," *Musical Courier*, 21 August 1912, p. 6.

20. Abell, "Berlin," *Musical Courier*, 25 September 1912, p. 5.

21. Rene DeVries, "Chicago," *Musical Courier*, 25 September 1912, p. 38.

22. George Fergusson, "On European Study," *Musical Courier*, 30 April 1913, p. 10.

23. Abell, "Berlin," *Musical Courier*, 16 March 1904, p. 6.

24. Interview with Reva Allman, June 1980.

25. Abell, "Berlin," *Musical Courier*, 19 June 1912, p. 5.

26. Evelyn Kaesmann, "London," *Musical Courier*, 25 September 1912, p. 1.

27. Ibid., 13 November 1912, p. 1.

28. Abell, "*Ariadne auf Naxos* at Stuttgart," *Musical Courier*, 13 November 1912, pp. 5-7.

29. Frank Patterson, "Paris," *Musical Courier*, 25 June 1913, p. 11.

30. Abell, "Berlin," *Musical Courier*, 15 January 1913, p. 46.

31. L. Anderson, "Brussels," *Musical Courier*, 8 January 1913, p. 51.

32. Ellen von Tideböhl, "Moscow," *Musical Courier*, 19 February 1913, p. 46.

33. Abell, "Berlin," *Musical Courier*, 19 February 1913, p. 6.

34. Patterson, "Paris," *Musical Courier*, 30 April 1913, p. 9.

35. Abell, "Retrospect of the Berlin Music Season," *Musical Courier*, 29 April 1914, pp. 36-38.

36. Lura Abell, "Lura Abell's Homecoming," *Musical Courier*, 16 September 1914, pp. 30-31.

37. F. Wight Neumann, "F. Wight Neumann Returns," *Musical Courier*, 16 September 1914, p. 36.

38. Ibid.

39. Interview with Josephine Harreld Love, August 1981.

CHAPTER 3

1. *New York Age*, 24 September 1914.

2. Ibid., 24 July 1920.

3. All newspaper items are from *Chicago Defender* unless otherwise noted.

4. *La Porte Daily Herald*, 15 October 1914.

5. *International Cyclopedia of Music and Musicians*, 10th ed. (New York: Dodd, Mead and Co., 1975), p. 320.

6. *Chicago Defender*, 5 January 1924.

7. *Chicago Defender* and *New York Age*, 1910-1914.

8. Interview with Josephine Harreld Love, August 1981.

9. Harrison to Locke, 2 May 1915. Alain Locke Papers, Manuscript Division, Moorland-Spingarn Research Center, Howard University.

10. Harrison to Locke, 4 March 1915. Alain Locke Papers.

11. *Chicago Defender*, 11 November 1916.

12. Harold C. Schonberg, *The Great Pianists* (New York: Simon and Schuster, 1963), p. 353.

13. Interview with Ralph Simpson, March 1980.

14. Reprinted in the *Chicago Defender*, 29 November 1919.

15. Maud Cuney Hare, *Negro Musicians and Their Music* (1936. Reprint. New York: Da Capo Press, 1974), p. 374.

16. Harrison to Locke, 2 May [1915]. Alain Locke Papers.

17. *New York Age*, 17 December 1914.

18. Interview with Frances Sampson Mask, November 1980.

19. Interview with Louise Fargher, May 1980.

20. *New York Age*, 12 June 1920.

21. Harrison to Locke, 12 June 1920. Alain Locke Papers.

22. Ibid.

23. Ibid.

24. Ibid., 28 April [no year].

25. Interview with Frederick Hall, June 1980.

26. Excerpt of press review used in Hazel Harrison's promotional literature.

27. *New York Age*, 31 July 1920.

28. *Chicago Defender*, 20 November 1920.

29. Harrison to Locke, May 9 [1922]. Alain Locke Papers.

30. Interview with Edward Boatner, January 1980.

31. *Chicago Defender*, 5 January 1924.

32. Harrison to Locke, 16 September [no year]. Alain Locke Papers.

33. Ibid., 26 January [no year].

34. Ibid., 19 June [1922].

35. Ibid., 5 November 1922.

36. Ibid., 1 November [no year].

37. *New York Age*, 15 March 1924.

38. *New York Age*, 5 April 1924.

39. Reprinted in *Chicago Defender*, 5 April 1924.

40. *Atlanta Journal*, 13 March 1927. Maybelle S. Wall, reviewer for the *Journal*, recalling the 1924 repeat performance.

41. *Chicago Defender*, 12 April 1924.

42. Ibid.

43. Ibid., 14 March 1925.

44. Harrison to Locke, 20 June 1925. Alain Locke Papers.

45. Interview with Florence Low Stoner, May 1980.

46. Interview with Alfonso Harrod, May 1980.

47. Harrison to Locke, 3 June [1925]. Alain Locke Papers.

48. Ibid., 20 June [1925].

49. Ibid., 8 November 1925.

50. Ibid., 1 January 1926.

51. Ibid.

52. Ibid., 11 January 1926.

53. Ibid.

54. Arthur Abell, "Impressions of Post-War Berlin," *Musical Courier*, 27 May 1926, p. 6.

55. *Chicago Defender*, 20 November 1926.

56. Ibid.

57. Hugo Leichtentritt, "Berlin Opera Produces Alban Berg's *Wozzeck*," *Musical Courier*, 7 January 1926, p. 5.

58. "Foreign News in Brief," *Musical Courier*, 11 February 1926, p. 6.

59. Ibid., 4 February 1926, p. 5.

60. Ibid.

61. Sebastian Jaspard, "Monte Carlo," *Musical Courier*, 11 March 1926, p. 5.

62. "Foreign News in Brief," *Musical Courier*, 15 April 1926, p. 22.

63. *Grove's Dictionary of Music and Musicians*, 5th ed., s.v. "Petri." (New York: St. Martin's Press, 1954).

64. *Musical Courier*, 8 April 1926, cover; 17 June 1926, p. 38.

65. "The Spirituals Come into Their Own," *Musical Courier*, 22 April 1926, p. 18; 19 August 1926, p. 18.

66. *Chicago Defender*, 30 April 1929.

67. Ibid.

68. Ibid., 1 February 1930.

69. David Stone, dean, School of Music, Temple University, to Cazort, 3 September 1980.

70. Harrison to Locke [November 1930]. Alain Locke Papers.

71. Interview with Josephine Harreld Love, August 1981.

CHAPTER 4

1. *Tuskegee Institute Bulletin*, 1931-1932, pp. 116-17.

2. Interview with William Mitchell, longtime Tuskegee resident, June 1980.

3. Ruth Ann Stewart, *Portia* (Garden City, N.Y.: Anchor Press, 1976), p. 71.

4. Interview with Portia Washington Pittman by Roy Hill, August 1974.

5. Stewart, p. 107.

6. Ralph Ellison, "The Little Man at Chehaw Station," *American Scholar* 47 (1977/78): 25-26.

7. *Tuskegee Messenger*, January 1932.

8. Interview with Josephine Harreld Love, August 1981.

9. *Tuskegee Institute Bulletin*, 1931-1932, pp. 119-20.

10. Interview with William Dawson, December 1979.

11. Interview with Mildred G. Hall, June 1980.

12. Telephone conversation with Mrs. Harry Richardson, former campus resident, July 1981.

13. Interview with William Dawson.

14. Ibid.

CHAPTER 5

1. Owen D. Nichols, secretary of the Board of Trustees, Howard University, to Hobson, 29 May 1981.

2. Interview with Lillian Mitchell Allen, professor emerita and retired head of the Department of Music Education, School of Music, Howard University, September 1981.

3. Carrie Burton Overton, "Howard University Conservatory and Miss Lulu Vere Childers As I Knew Them," *Semi-Centennial of the School of Music, College of Fine Arts, Howard University, Washington, D.C., 1914-1964*, 1964, p. 3.

4. *Howard University School of Music Bulletin*, 1936-1937, p. 8.

5. Interview with Lillian Allen.

6. *Howard Alumni Journal*, Spring 1937, p. 5.

7. Interview with Lillian Allen.

8. Ibid.

9. Harrison to Goins [n.d.], Gregoria Goins Papers, Manuscript Division, Moorland-Spingarn Research Center, Howard University.

10. *Howard University School of Music Bulletin, 1936-1937*, p. 14.

11. Interview with Frances White Hughes, June 1981.

12. Interview with Robert Earl Anderson, June 1981.

13. Interview with Frances White Hughes.

14. The authors are grateful to former Harrison students for these comments gleaned from conversations, 1981.

15. Interview with Frances White Hughes.

16. Interview with Robert Earl Anderson.

17. Interview with Hermine Johnigan, May 1980.

18. Telephone interview with Sterling W. Thomas, July 1981.

19. Telephone interview with Chester Rowlett, July 1981.

20. Interview with Robert Earl Anderson.

21. David Stone, dean, School of Music, Temple University, to Cazort, 3 September 1980.

22. Interview with Robert Earl Anderson.

23. Interview with Alfonso Harrod, May 1980.

24. *Howard University School of Music Annual Report*, 1954-1955, p. 16.

25. Ibid., 1938-1939, p. 6.

26. Ibid., 1942-1943, p. 13.

27. Ibid., 1944-1945, p. 11.

28. Ibid., 1938-1939, p. 16.

29. *La Porte Herald-Argus*, 1 April 1938.

30. Ibid.

31. Ibid.

32. Ibid.

33. *Washington News*, 16 November 1938.

34. *Washington Times*, 16 November 1938.

35. Doris E. McGinty, "The Washington Conservatory of Music and School of Expression," *The Black Perspective in Music*, 7 (1979): 66.

36. Ibid., p. 67.

37. *Washington Star*, 22 October 1939.

38. McGinty, p. 68.

39. Interview with Alfonso Harrod.

40. *Annual Reports*, 1946-1947, p. 75; 1949-1950, p. 35.

41. National Association of Negro Musicians, Souvenir Program, 30th Anniversary, August 1949 [p. 11].

42. Ibid. [p. 13].

43. *Howard University Bulletin*, February 1950.

44. Interview with Alfonso Harrod.

45. *Annual Report*, 1953-1954, p. 72.

46. Interview with Ralph Simpson, March 1980.

47. These editions are among those in the Hazel Harrison Papers, Moorland-Spingarn Research Center, Howard University.

48. Fosdick to Harrison, 28 October 1955. Hazel Harrison Papers.

49. Ibid.

50. Wroten to Hobson, 6 January 1982.

51. Letter circulated to Harrison students in New York City.

52. Trenholm to Harrison, 14 October 1957. Hazel Harrison Papers.

53. Wroten to Hobson, 6 January 1982.

CHAPTER 6

1. Interview with Mildred Hall, June 1980.

2. Interview with Althea Thomas, June 1980.

3. Interview with Grennetta Simpson, June 1980.

4. Interview with Ralph Simpson, March 1980.

5. Interview with Paul Gary, August 1980.

6. Ibid.

7. Interview with Ralph Simpson.

8. Ibid.

9. Interview with Grennetta Simpson.

10. Interview with Ralph Simpson.

11. Ibid.

12. Interview with Minnie Scott, June 1980.

13. Interview with Grennetta Simpson.

14. Interview with Ralph Simpson.

15. Interview with Minnie Scott.

16. Ibid.

17. Interview with Elizabeth Foster, June 1980.

18. Interview with Ralph Simpson.

19. Portia Washington Pittman to Roy Hill, 23 January 1962.

20. Interview with Reva Allman, June 1980.

21. Interview with Mildred Hall.

22. Interview with Benjamin Ward, June 1980.

23. Ibid.

24. Interview with Minnie Scott.

25. Interview with Elizabeth Foster.

CHAPTER 7

1. Harrison to Foster, Christmas [1965].
2. Ibid., 28 January 1966.
3. Interview with Benjamin Ward, June 1980.
4. Harrison to Allman [n.d.].
5. Interview with Benjamin Ward.
6. Roy L. Hill, *Booker T's Child* (Newark: McDaniel Press, 1974), p. 80.
7. Interview with Reva Allman, June 1980.
8. Harrison to Florence Andrew, 24 June 1967.
9. Hill, p. 81.

BIBLIOGRAPHY

I. PRIMARY SOURCES

Gregoria Goins Papers, Manuscript Division, Moorland-Spingarn Research Center, Howard University.

Hazel Harrison Papers, Manuscript Division, Moorland-Spingarn Research Center, Howard University.

Alain Locke Papers, Manuscript Division, Moorland-Spingarn Research Center, Howard University.

II. SECONDARY SOURCES

Abdul, Raoul. *Blacks in Classical Music*. New York: Dodd, Mead and Co., 1977.

Brawley, Benjamin. *Negro Builders and Heroes*. Chapel Hill: University of North Carolina Press, 1937.

Chicago Defender, 1910-1930.

Grove's Dictionary of Music and Musicians. 5th ed. Edited by Eric Bloom. 9 vols. New York: St. Martin's Press, 1954.

Hare, Maud Cuney. *Negro Musicians and Their Music*. 1936. Reprint. New York: Da Capo Press, 1974.

Hill, Roy L. *Booker T's Child: The Life and Times of Portia Marshall Washington Pittman*. Newark: McDaniel Press, 1974.

International Cyclopedia of Music and Musicians, 10th ed. New York: Dodd, Mead and Co., 1975.

La Porte Daily Herald, 1895-1912.

La Porte Herald-Argus, 26 June 1925; 1 April 1938.

Love, Josephine Harreld. "Hazel Lucile Harrison." In *Notable American Women, The Modern Period: A Biographical Directory*, edited by Barbara Sicherman, Carol Green, Ilene Kantrov, and Harriette Walder, pp. 317-19. Cambridge, Mass.: Harvard University Press, 1980.

Musical Courier, 1904, 1911-1914, 1926.

The New Grove Dictionary of Music and Musicians. Edited by Stanley Sadie. 20 vols. London: Macmillan, 1980.

New York Age, 1910-1930.

Rubinstein, Arthur. *My Young Years*. New York: W. W. Norton and Co., 1971.

Schonberg, Harold C. *The Great Pianists*. New York: Simon and Schuster, 1963.

Southall, Geneva. *Blind Tom: The Post Civil-War Enslavement of a Black Musical Genius*. Minneapolis: Challenge Productions, 1979.

Southern, Eileen. *The Music of Black Americans: A History*. New York, W. W. Norton and Co., 1971.

Stewart, Ruth Ann. *Portia: The Life of Portia Washington Pittman, the Daughter of Booker T. Washington*. Garden City, N.Y.: Anchor Press, 1976.

Tuskegee Messenger, 1930-1936.

INDEX

About the Authors

JEAN CAZORT is Associate Librarian at Fisk University and has contributed an article on genealogical research for *Ethnic Genealogy: A Research Guide* (edited by Jessie C. Smith), soon to be published by Greenwood Press.

CONSTANCE TIBBS HOBSON, a former student of Harrison, is Professor of Music Theory in the College of Arts and Sciences at Howard University in Washington and is herself a solo pianist and accompanist.